Agaphileros C

8 Movements to the Love of a Lifetime.

By

Roger A. Watson

Copyright © 2015 Roger A. Watson

All rights reserved.

ISBN: 0989389634

ISBN-13: 978-09893896-3-1

All rights reserved. No portion to be reproduced without prior written permission of the publisher.

All material authored and created by Roger A. Watson unless noted.

Published by Agaphileros LLC.

All scripture quotations marked AMP are taken from The Amplified Bible © 1954, 1958, 1962, 1964, 1965, 1987 by the Lockman Foundation. All rights reserved.

All scripture quotations marked NKJV are from The Holy Bible, New King James Version ©1979, 1980, 1982. All rights reserved.

Printed in the United States of America

Impact Guarantee

Dear Reader, I was guided by the Holy Spirit to include this *Impact Guarantee* for your eyes and your understanding. We (the Holy Spirit and I) guarantee that this material *will* impact the way you think about your current and future relationships, Impact how you now view your previous relationships, impact how you speak to certain people in your life, impact your prayer time, impact your decision making process, impact how you see God and His word or impact a part of your life not mentioned here. However, if you totally disagree with every thought or idea, if you have read the entire book, if there is no damage to it and you do not have anything written in it, then contact us by phone or email and we will inform you as to where to send it. We will reimburse you your purchase cost for every printed copy you return. Contact must be within 40 days from purchase with proof of purchase. However, if you have been impacted by this book, please let us know in 40 words or less by phone or by email. We would appreciate it very much. Visit www.agaphileros.com for contact information.

Dedication

This book is dedicated to those who believe in real love. Let's keep on loving until our final breath because love is the greatest *because*.

And Jacob served seven years for Rachel; and they seemed to him but a few days **because** *of the love he had for her.*

Genesis 29:20 Amplified Bible

The Flow

Introduction. p10

M1: If Eros is an Island then let me explore. p14
Come to my island. The island is all yours. Know the resources. To my brothers. To my sisters. To the both of you. Eros experiences: failures and enhancements. Explore your island.

M2: Permanent vs Temporary (Reloaded). p28
Never Neverland. The Agaphileroso and the Temporary. The Agaphilerosas and the Temporary. How does a Permanent refine their character? How does a Permanent think? How does a Permanent build?

M3: New wine in old wineskins. p46
It's all about relationships. Jesus is the wedge. The old vs the new. Stretching your skin. Has anyone seen my collagen? The truth about protein. Sweet tooth. Ready, set, process. Practice makes perfect protein. A whole new world. If you build it they will come. We can! You can!

M4: The X Factor. p68
What is the X Factor? Only God knows the BIG picture. Not my will but yours, Oh Lord. Prepared for the X Factor.

M5: A word to the agaphilerosa. p78
Genesis 2 for the agaphilerosa. Leave e-v-i-l alone and l-i-v-e. Genesis 24 for the agaphilerosa. Psalms 16:11. Relationship killers. Qualities to look for in a husband. Grace nuggets.

M6: A word to the agaphileroso. p112
Teachable, reachable, reliable and keepable. Cut it off! Genesis 2 for the agaphileroso. The food, the water, the money and the life. Leave the e-v-i-l alone and l-i-v-e. Genesis 24 for the agaphileroso. Psalms 16:11. Relationship killers. Qualities to look for in a wife. Grace nuggets.

M7: Becoming equally yoked. p142
Quality versus cheap. Characteristics of quality people and their relationships. Confession of quality. We have a champion: Love! 8 Foundational Principles of an agaphileros marriage.

M8: Sex and the Sacrifice. p168
Sexual sacrifice. Soul ties. Waiting on the Right one. To the ladies. To the men. Celebrate her. Sexual healing in the Honeymoon.

Conclusion: Pt 2. The Beginning. p184
Creating and inventing. The love of a lifetime. Believe and begin again. Why? Why Now? Why You? The Promise is possible.

References: p192

THE BONUS p194

Kiss

Winning

You inspire me

You had me at hello

We win!

A vow for 2 please

INTRODUCTION

When you say yes to what is temporary, you say no to what is permanent.

Hello and welcome to the 3rd project of Agaphileros. This particular project is a continuation of Agaphileros B and they share many similarities. You will notice that Movement 9 from "B" is Movement 1 in "C". Whereas "B" concentrated on all of Agaphileros with a particular emphasis on agape, "C" is focused entirely on eros. The Conclusion represents the conclusion of both projects. Finally, I have added a Reloaded Movement on Temporaries versus Permanents, 5 poems and a vow from "A". You now have your "pelau" (a mix-up of items), as we call it in Trinidad and Tobago.

It is easy to speak to the majority of people in the world about eros because most everyone wants to get intimate with someone of the opposite sex on a regular basis. God designed us for intimacy; we are wired for it, and it really does not matter if you are a born again Christian, a Muslim, a Catholic, a Buddhist, a Hindu, an atheist, Black, Caucasian, Oriental, Indian or Hispanic, you want intimacy. We may not agree on many things but one thing is for sure, all nations, ethnic groups and religions have experienced eros.

But for many younger people and some seasoned singles it has become a struggle to speak about intimacy much less to enjoy it the right way. Some even struggle to form strong relationships. I spent a considerable amount of time coming up with the 8 movements that you are about to read and they are all designed to prepare you to enjoy the love of a lifetime when it shows up.

One of the many books I read this year was a book by Dr. Gary Chapman called, "The 5 love Languages". I suggest you get a copy for yourself and one to share. By the time I read the book, I had completed over 95% of Agaphileros B and C. I found that although I did not know about love languages in 1997, I had begun to discover what Agaphileros was and what the 5 love languages were through being married to Jessy. I can now say that her primary love language was quality time. Thinking back to some of our arguments I now realize that she often complained about the quality time that I was not giving to her. We were speaking different languages.

The amazing thing is that the Holy Spirit knew that we loved each other and helped me to realize that I had to work, sacrifice and change in order to save the relation-ship. Without knowing it then, I began to speak all 5 primary love languages to Jessy until I became fluent in them, and then spoke a few others for good measure.

That is what Agaphileros is all about, giving the other person whatever it is that they need in order to feel your love, even if you give them more than they need. What I did to her triggered a love language reaction in her and she began to reciprocate. The language barrier was removed.

Giving your love to someone else at that level is an almost impossible task for anyone who is lazy, selfish and stubborn because those traits are diametrically opposed to work, sacrifice and change. It is far easier to run to a divorce lawyer than it is to renew your thinking, isn't it? And indeed, a renewed mind is the first thing that you need in order to win. "8 Movements" takes you through a process of mind renewing activities to enable you to get to doing the work, making the sacrifices and initiating the changes that you must, in order to win.

Yet, what many people do not realize, is that God never asks you to go it alone in marriage. He does not desire to be a silent partner, but rather, an active 24/7 vocally participating member of your ship. Nobody wants you to win more than your heavenly Father, nobody. That is why He provided books like Dr. Chapman's and other resources to help you to get better. Most importantly, you have the word of God and the Holy Spirit to educate and assist you. Beloved, you will not fail.

For those who believe that they have found the love of a lifetime, there is more information in here to assist you in keeping what you have found. Use this project as a reference tool, a workbook, or whatever you need it to be. Take your time, read slowly and meditate on what you read. Eros is not only designed for sprints but more often than not its design reveals an inclination toward marathons. So take your positions on the starting line, get ready, get set and let's go.

MOVEMENT 1

If Eros is an Island then let me explore

Some scientists say that everything in the universe is comprised of little things called strings. That is called the String Theory. Small things make big things. Do not despise small things because you need them to build bigger things. Find the little things. Explore.

Come to my island

If Agape is like an ocean then Eros is like an island. "*No man is an island*", a poem by John Donne, has captured that phrase and we use it widely today to let individuals know that they need other people. That is true, we need other people in order to fulfil our part in the entire scheme of life. You need parents to birth you, teachers to teach you, managers to work you, leaders to motivate you, and someone to love you. We all have that God given urge to be loved. You also need other people so that you can express yourself in them, for them and to them to express love, unity, family and so on. You cannot survive well without others.

Yet I would like to look at mankind in a different light for a moment and add to Mr. Donne's view of things. When it comes to Eros, see yourself and your lifetime lover as islands because eros is all about intimacy and you get to assist in making their island an island of intimacy. He has placed you both in the middle of Agape, the ocean of love. You have been set apart by your creator *for* someone that will help you, and *from* those that will hurt you. Contained within you are all the things that they will need and vice versa.

My island is for my Agaphilerosa and I have ready and on hand what she needs to be delighted and satisfied. Do you not know that she has everything that I need to be delighted and satisfied as well? Your island is the same, and just as an island is never untouched by the ocean, Eros is never untouched by Agape. You are an island, touched by and surrounded by an ocean of love.

Before you can get to an island you must navigate the ocean. Once you understand Agape and all its intricacies, you can happily arrive at Eros. You may choose to arrive by boat, submarine, canoe, scuba equipment, a raft or by swimming but as the song by Oleta Adams says, get there if you can. Many people may have to take a longer journey there because God knows they need some more love education before they hurt someone else.

In addition, some people may have been through a lot of hurt and people have almost destroyed their island. Some have been abused sexually, some may have had their innocence taken at an early age and some may have had their island desecrated and decimated by so-called loved ones and it has affected them up to today. That might be you. I have good news for you today. God is in the rebuilding, reconstructing and redeeming business as well. Somehow, what the devil meant for evil, God can turn it around and make it good for you but you will have to trust His work in you.

The island is all yours

Whether you are on your way to someone else's island or someone is on the way to your island, you have to understand islands and how they work to gain the best benefit from it. You benefit best from what you understand the best and utilize the most. See that island as something that God has prepared *for* you because He did. Allow me to repeat myself, He prepared the island just for you. Have some faith in God and believe that He knows exactly what you need for a lifetime of love.

We often focus on how God brought Eve to Adam and the fact that Adam did all the speaking when they first met. I suppose he was blown away at her appearance. However, don't you think that Eve was also very happy to see her man for the first time? The first person she saw was a hunk created just for her, I mean specifically crafted and proportioned for her every satisfaction.

Ladies, I am talking to you about encountering a hunk and not some junk, looking good and not acting hood, capable, able and mentally stable, full of life and ready for a wife, can step up to the plate and won't be late, striving and thriving to make a better living, not bringing any drama and not causing any trauma. After he meets you he is done with the rest because he has been blessed with the best and can pass any test without giving in to the stress of the dress.

All of that is for you my sister and to solidify it totally, he understands what it means to love God for real. If a man really learns to love God and practices what he has learned he will not have any problem loving you the way you need to be loved. I could bet that when Eve saw Adam she was smiling from ear to ear, breathing somewhat heavier and getting hot flashes.

And think about this, she had no other women for her to compete with, no sports to talk about, no television to watch, no nightly news to see, no technology to distract him, no social media to update, no distractions at work, no "toys" to play with, no "boys" to hang with, no in-laws to deal with, absolutely nothing but her as the object of his attention (once he was finished working in the garden of course. A man needs to work). Every night was her night. He was all hers. That relationship was the first Agaphileros relationship in recorded history. That was God's design and that was the way it was supposed to be.

Could you imagine Adam's delight in seeing Eve? Oh how his heart rate must have increased. Guys, you know how we can be. You know how we did when we first saw our wives. Her lips, hips and fingertips were examined and the data uploaded into our CPUs. No flaws when she walked toward us and perfection when she passed on by. We caught her scent in the wind and it began to intoxicate our minds. When our eyes met there was an instant connection, a strong detection that our selection was a reflection of the summation of our views of perfection wrapped up in the sweetest complexion who we then lovingly gave our protection, our attention and our affection for the duration of the age of satisfaction until the completion of our mission. She was fine, inside and out. Amen.

In reality, we were probably jumping up and praising God on the inside while trying to hold it together on the outside. Like puppy dogs enjoying the warm hug of a child who loves us, our tails probably couldn't stop wagging and we didn't want to let her go. Sometimes, if the connection was a long awaited one, there may have been tears of joy flowing within us. Smiling on the inside while crying on the outside = joy. Sorrow is usually the opposite of that. And there is no shame when the tears are visible.

There is no shame when you have been blessed by God with an island that is ripe for exploration and unlimited discovery. As all wise husbands know, we can spend a lifetime discovering what is contained within our wives, never obtaining full discovery but glad that we were given the opportunity to explore. Are you a wise husband, brother?

This is your island. It has been prepared and preserved for you and you alone. God designed it like the Garden of Eden; a place of delight and satisfaction. If you trust Him you will find everything that you will ever need for a lifetime relationship in it. If you treat it right it will blossom and bloom for you all year long. If you take your time with it, it will supply you with desire and pleasure for the rest of your days. You will not need to leave this island, ever. So set up shop, take your time and discover what is yours, all yours. (That sounded like a commercial for a time share didn't it)?

When you finally arrive on the island, chart it well. Take your time to explore and do some reconnaissance. To do reconnaissance is to do a *general* survey of a region, followed by a very *detailed* survey of that region. Sounds like dating doesn't it? Detailed surveys can take a very long time depending on the targeted region being surveyed. No rush, you have a lifetime. Understand its habitat and its make-up. What are the fruit trees that grow there? What vegetables are buried in it? What type of soil does it contain? Are there any hills and valleys? What areas can be visited often and which ones maybe not as often? Are there any precious metals and rare gems within? What is its most comfortable temperature and what is its most productive season? What makes it bloom with beauty and what makes it cringe with unfruitfulness? Explore its forestry, its foliage and its functionality.

Know the resources

Brothers and sisters, the islands are not self-contained. A lot of their resources come from the ocean. Whether these resources are within the ocean itself or travel across the ocean from other places, you need to know the ocean and the source of the supplies in order to benefit *from* the island. You also need to understand the island to be a benefit *to* it. You have to be a blessing and an asset to the island or you will become a curse and a liability to it.

Beloved, you are going to have to be a resource to their island. God has equipped you to be one of its suppliers. How do you supply their island? Firstly, find out what they need and then see what it is that you have to give. Chances are that if he/she is the one there will be compatibility there. They may need to be spoken gently to and you are someone that speaks gently to people. They may need someone who is a good decision maker and you are pretty good at making decisions. They may have impulsive tendencies and you are pretty level headed. If the both of you think like suppliers coming in to the relationship you will gain access to marital success at a much faster rate.

God is also a resource to the islands seeing that He created them. The Creator always knows why He created something or someone and He will always have a supply for it to be all that it can be. The Love Manual is one of the resources He has supplied, the Holy Spirit is a resource, angels are also a resource and good counselors are a resource as well. Staying in contact with the creator as a team is also a good way to maintain healthy supply levels. You can do this through praying, meditating, declaring and confessing some things. Spending time in the Love Manual cannot be substituted in any way for success in your relationship. The more you study and execute the instructions in the Manual the more you prepare yourself to properly explore your lover's island.

To my brothers

Many people *never* take the time to develop an intimate knowledge of the island they have been blessed with, especially my brothers. Bro, yes you, eros is all about intimacy. How can you be intimate with your wife if you do not take the time to get to know her? Also, do not let your momentum for exploration wane over time. Remember how you first noticed her? Keep on noticing her, keep on giving her attention because she needs it from you. Intimacy, some say is **in-to-me-see**. If that is the case then there is only one way to see into her; you have to stop looking at others and focus on her. Not to nit-pick about flaws but to compliment and encourage what is there, and to develop what needs to be developed. You will be amazed what steady heartfelt compliments will do to your intimacy level and hers as well.

One thing I enjoyed doing to Jessy was melting her with my words or actions. Have you ever seen a woman melt? It made me feel like 10 feet tall, and I am not even 6 feet tall. (Actually I am only 5 feet 7 inches at this time). A melted woman is at her peak intimate moment. This is when the weather is perfect over the island, the trees are all bearing sweet fruit and there is a cool breeze blowing over the landscape. You get a chance to make your special island a melted paradise if you speak the right words at the right time and do the right things at the right moment. If you constantly practice this, if you think before you speak, if you never stop being an explorer and if you utilize your resources, then you will become a master melter.

By the way, every island comes equipped with a volcano on it. Be careful not to stimulate the volcano. It is one of the things you should learn very quickly how *not* to do. Learn the triggers. Learn and study what words and what actions can cause the lava to rise. As an explosion survivor, trust me when I tell you that you do *not* want to trigger an eruption. Eruptions end Eros. And all the ladies said, Amen.

Brothers, marriage does not mean settle down into the *marriage routine*. On the contrary, marriage means explore more and more, dig deeper and deeper, love richer and richer, reach further and further and build higher and higher. You do not ever cease until the final breath is breathed. Spontaneity is good for the island. Take a stroll up a mountain one day, go to a beach the next day, and travel into the forest the day after that. This is the day that the Lord (love) has made. Do not let it be a dull and boring day. Even when she might not be feeling her best, practice cuddling, because it may be all that she needs. When she is having a tough day, change your schedule and surprise her with your presence. It will make her day. You do not have to be rich or be the most creative person on the planet. You just have to keep giving your best effort. Good women can tell when the effort is there and when it is sincere.

Having a growing relationship with the island is essential because knowledge is buried all over the island just for you. Have you ever been on a treasure hunt? Do you know how to read her map? Study the legend that explains the map. Ask questions when appropriate. It truly amazes me to see how much knowledge can be garnered from a woman if you spend the time to get the information from her.

Sometimes in the Love Manual it talks about a man knowing his wife and all we hear is "sex". The Hebrew word for "knew" does not give the word "sex" as one of the meanings of the word. To think that "knew", "know" or "eros" is sex is to miss the entire point of the message of true love. To "know" your wife means to find out and discern, to know by experience, to consider and to gain revelation. That is just some of the meanings of the word.

She is designed for much more than sex. She is designed and built for intimacy and a host of other great things. Every time you discover something on the island you can increase the intimacy level. Discovery is the door to see more than you did before.

Concentrate and focus on discovering who she is and not on what she can do for you. Women love to be discovered. As I mentioned in Agaphileros A, you have to make love to her mind before you can properly make love to her body. Do not focus so much on below the waist that you neglect to put in the work above the neck. Eros begins in the head first.

To my sisters

This section will not be long because intimacy for a man is not usually very complicated. We look for what we like and when we see it we go after it. Most of us are very simple like that. We are very visual so your island must be handled with exquisite care. Some men do not like islands that are flashy and fancy but some do. However, be careful that you are not baiting the wrong type of man to your island. Unmarried women that are ready to be married usually decorate their islands a bit differently than women that are out for a good time. Are you decorating your island for a temporary or for a permanent? Are you trying to attract a gigolo or a lifetime lover? There is a difference.

Now, when you finally hook up with the one that you can experience eros with, begin to explore his potential. Every island has potential and God has equipped you to develop your husband's potential. This usually comes naturally over time to women that have lived a while, have been through some challenges, have had some children and have been in a serious relationship before. If you are new to this, have no fear. You have an innate ability to figure this out. Spend time in prayer, in the Love Manual and most of all becoming selfless and these together will propel you forward into great moments in eros.

To the both of you

Depending on how well you explore each other's islands you will open the door to wonderful moments of sexual encounters where the both of you will be satisfied. However, sex today is more of an industry than a part of an institution, more of a choice rather than a covenant. I still believe that sex within the confines of the covenant of marriage affects the path of the relationship, protects the purpose of the relationship and respects the purity of the relationship.

Sex outside of the confines of the covenant of marriage

still affects the path of the relationship but provides little to no protection for the relationship and disrespects the purity of the relationship. There are just some parts of the island that you should refrain from until the covenant is ready to be sealed with the sacrifice on the altar (discussed in another part of this project).

Because being a virgin is now considered old fashioned many people steer clear of it as if it is a dishonor to be called a virgin. However, being a virgin is a blessing. What greater gift can you bring to a wedding ceremony than an untouched island, one that has never been invaded or inhabited? I know it is rare and I am not trying to bring conviction to anyone because my island was not untouched when I married Jessy, but if your island is pure and clean, hold on to that. It is the one regret that I brought to our marriage. You will avoid a lot of drama and trauma by waiting to be explored on your wedding night rather than having open house on your island every other weekend.

Eros experiences: failures and enhancements

Finally beloved, let us look at some things that cause eros failures and some things that enhance eros experiences. The number 1 issue that causes eros failures can be seen in your bedroom, bathroom, and hallway, and sometimes even next to your front door. You live with it, eat with it, sleep with it, shower with it, work with it, play with it, laugh with it, cry with it and pretty much do everything with it. The number one issue that causes eros failures is what you see daily in the mirror and experience life with 24/7; you. An eros failure begins with you and you are the one person that you can work on.

Brothers, it is difficult for a woman to become intimate with you if all she feels is that you are working on her and never on yourself. Sisters, it is difficult for a man to be intimate with you if he feels like you are belittling and dominating him and not working on yourself. Isn't it amazing that if you meet someone who was married, engaged or dating someone that they have broken up with that the other person was at fault almost 100% of the time? How is it that we are fortunate to always meet the person who loves the right way and never love the wrong way? We must be *lucky* like that. However, I have lived long enough to realize that there are always about 3 sides to a story: his, hers and God's.

Why do we do that? Why do we "dog out" the people we used to be with? We often are trying to *defend our pride* so we find their mistakes and tell our side of the story. Next time forget your pride and find your own mistakes, then tell the rest of the story. We also try to *hurt their image* because we are hurting from the break up and we want them to hurt as well. Next time, get over yourself and speak good or not at all. Sometimes, we are *just plain angry* and want to make them look like the devil himself or just plain stupid for breaking up with us. The truth be told, we all have things to work on in order to be better people so learn to control your emotions and do not let it control you.

And if the person that you just met only has negative things to say about their exes, why in heaven's name would you give them any time to build agaphileros with you? Do you not realize that if your relationship ends that they will be talking about you the very same way to the next person? However, if they can fairly point out their mistakes and errors and are able to tell you about the work, sacrifices and changes that they have made, then listen and observe. I am talking truth here and not a pick up line to make you a statistic or a sob story to get you hooked so that they can relieve you of your finances or something else. That is why you need the Holy Spirit and some time for things to be proved out. If they are hiding the truth and feeding a lie, eventually the lie will explode (see M5).

The good thing is that the number 1 thing that causes an eros failure is the same thing that enhances it; you. I am telling you beloved, if you take the time to do the necessary work for intimacy, make the obvious sacrifices for it and initiate the much needed changes it deserves, you will be the greatest island keeper that your lover has ever known. Brothers, your potential will explode upon the earth and a man with the right island is unstoppable. She will pull some things out of you that you may not even have known was there. Sisters, you will become the envy of all your girlfriends, co-workers and social media as you have to keep explaining why you look so happy all the time.

Good women are willing to fight for love like this and real men, like Jesus, are willing to give their lives for the woman they love. That means the both of you have the power to make a stand for each other to the last breath so stop looking at your lover as just another person. That person is an island designed just for you, with resources from everywhere, in need of the right type of explorer to do some work to create an island of intimacy.

Explore your island

If you are married and you have not been intimate with your spouse in a while, start tonight. Depending on where you are, you can begin right at this very moment. What do they like on a day, a night or a time like this? Find out. What have you stopped doing that you know they love so much? Do your best again. If it's been a while then you may have to don your Indiana Jones outfit or your Lara Croft leather attire and make preparations for exploration. You can do it, they deserve it and the world needs it.

Take Aways M1

- ✓ When it comes to Eros, see yourself and your lifetime lover as islands because Eros is all about intimacy and you get to assist in making their island an island of intimacy.

- ✓ You have been set apart by your creator *for* someone that will help you, and *from* those that will hurt you.

- ✓ You benefit best from what you understand the best and utilize the most.

- ✓ If a man really learns to love God and practices what he has learned he will not have any problem loving you the way you need to be loved.

- ✓ Brothers and sisters, the islands are not self-contained.

- ✓ You have to be a blessing and an asset to the island or you will become a curse and a liability to it.

- ✓ A melted woman is at her peak intimate moment.

- ✓ Every island comes equipped with a volcano on it. Be careful not to stimulate the volcano. Eruptions end Eros.

- ✓ Marriage means explore more and more, dig deeper and deeper, love richer and richer, reach further and further and build higher and higher.

- ✓ Good women can tell when the effort is there and when it is sincere.

- ✓ To think that "knew", "know" or "eros" is sex is to miss the entire point of the message of true love. To "know" your wife means to find out and discern, to know by experience, to consider and to gain revelation.

- ✓ Sisters, spend time in prayer, in the Love Manual and most of all becoming selfless and these together will propel you forward into great moments in eros.

- ✓ Sex within the confines of the covenant of marriage affects the path of the relationship, protect the purpose of the relationship and respects the purity of the relationship.

- ✓ What greater gift can you bring to a wedding ceremony than an untouched island, one that has never been invaded or inhabited? You will avoid a lot of drama and trauma by waiting to be explored on your wedding night rather than having open house on your island every other weekend.

- ✓ The #1 thing that causes an eros failure is the same thing that enhances it; you. Take the time to do the necessary work for intimacy, make the obvious sacrifices for it and initiate the much needed changes it deserves.

- ✓ Good women are willing to fight for love like this and real men, like Jesus, are willing to give their lives for the woman they love.

MOVEMENT 2

Permanent vs Temporary (Reloaded)

Never give your permanent things to temporary people.

Never Neverland

"What are the permanent things," you ask? Permanent things are those things in your life that should be accessed only by a person who qualifies as a *permanent* person for you. Who is a permanent person? A permanent person is someone who God brings into your life that He has specifically chosen for you so that you can enjoy the love of a lifetime. In that case, a *temporary* is someone who is *not* that person. So if God has given you a permanent person, surely He will also bless you with all that you will need to love the person in the right way so that the both of you can thrive in the relationship.

You are also a permanent person when your thinking has changed and begins to line up with what is right about love. This means that you have been through some trials and errors but have not quit or given up on love. You know that any good relationship will take work, require sacrifice and demand changes. You are a permanent if you are constantly working on your horizontal and vertical relationships. You are no longer interested in being selfish, rather, selflessness is constantly on your agenda. If you are a permanent, and you also understand what a permanent person is supposed to act like, it will help you to avoid the behavioral dramas of temporaries. It is in light of this that I now offer Never Neverland.

Never give up a permanent person for a temporary person. This is a common mistake made by people who are immature and unstable in relationships. If you walk out on a permanent person you walk out on the best thing that could ever happen to you. It would be far better for you to have never met a permanent person than to have one and walk out on them. Many men have been drawn away and enticed by temporaries, more so than women. You can ruin the very fabric of your future by yielding to the temptation of a temporary, not to mention the future of your family.

The cost of that selfish transaction is staggering when estimated. The real cost of a broken home is that it affects every community, every country and ultimately, the entire world. Fatherless homes, single parent homes and unsupervised kids, may lead to a lack of balanced discipline, social problems, psychological issues, and mental health problems, which in turn may cause many children to end up in some type of institution or in the so-called "system". As usual, the children pay the heaviest price. Beloved, learn to just say no to that Neverland.

Never hook up to a temporary while waiting for a permanent to show up. Do not become unequally yoked together with a temporary if you are a permanent waiting on a permanent. On the other hand, if you are a temporary, feel free to hook up with a temporary and do not waste the time of a permanent. Permanents do not want to waste time because they believe in productivity. If you like to waste time, it is probably because you are a temporary. Time is one of the 3 main commodities (time, resources and energy) that we are given in life and people that are permanents know that every second counts.

Be not weary in permanent-waiting, for in due season they shall show up and you will reap if you faint not. It is not so much that God does not have one for you, as much as it is that you may be still operating as a temporary yourself, while learning the permanent lifestyle. Do not be afraid. God has a permanent for you. Just keep on growing into your permanent status. It will not be in vain. They are always worth the wait.

Never try to hold permanent conversations with temporary-minded people. Conversations by a permanent with a temporary will eventually become the equivalent of speaking to a brick wall. As a permanent, that will frustrate you. No matter how much you speak about long term items, they will always bring it back to the short term or to things that matter very little. You may be trying very hard to bring them into some measure of permanency but soon and very soon, their temporary mentality will begin to show up. So in order to keep from pulling out your hair and having to invest in a weave, a toupee or a helmet, reserve permanent conversations for permanent people.

All permanents recognize the power of words. They do not just speak words, they covenant. Every word out of the mouth of a permanent person is covenant based and love infused. A conversation between 2 permanent lovers is bliss in and of itself, whereas a conversation between 2 temporary lovers is painful on the ears.

Never build anything permanent with a temporary person. It is inevitable that the life that you build together will collapse. Do not be surprised when the joints of "being in love" begin to come loose and the nails of "bliss" no longer hold the structure together. Many women, have fallen for the smooth talking temporaries who eventually left them with the baby, the bills and the blame. Seems like he just said hello the other day and now it's all about the goodbye.

Now you have a child, and children tend to be permanent fixtures in your life. You also have the bills for what you both tried to build that fell apart. (Creditors do not care if your relationships do not work out). Next comes the court system which has to intervene to assist you to legally obtain financial resources from a temporary person. Who are you going to blame for that?

Permanents focus on building things that last, whereas temporaries focus on building things fast. Permanents like building with quality materials, but temporaries build with anything they can get their hands on. Permanents use blueprints, whereas temporaries leave footprints as they walk away. Permanents do not mind waiting on what is right, but temporaries believe that it is their right not to wait for anything. Permanents believe in developing themselves, however, temporaries believe in pleasing themselves.

Sadly at times, a temporary actually gets to the marriage altar with a permanent. They play the game well enough and say all the right things while in the pursuit of marriage, yet know full well that they are not intending to build anything permanent with the other person. A temporary clothed in permanent clothing is a dangerous person, especially if you have built anything with them. They can become your worst nightmare.

Now, while we are on the topic of nightmare I also advise that permanents never hang around people who like to throw tantrums and throw things. It is one thing to be angry and not sin, but it is another thing to be angry and hurt people or destroy property. To sin is to miss the mark or the standard that the Love Manual has instructed for behavior. If the person in your life is not taking authority over their behavior to improve themselves, chances are that you may be dealing with a temporary in permanent clothing.

When you realize that you are involved with a temporary you will have to make one of two decisions. You will have to decide to either keep the relationship as is, for whatever reason you choose, or you will yield to good sense and stop building with that person. You will have to choose at some point: yes or no. Just remember, when you say yes to who is temporary, you say no to who is permanent.

The Agaphileroso and the Temporary

Agaphilerosos, (men who practice agaphileros), be on the lookout for temporaries. Solomon talks about the lure of the strange woman (very temporary) and the man caught up in her schemes in Proverbs 5:1-14, 20-23. She sounds incredibly determined to destroy the man, but thank God that He always gives us an alternative to temporaries.

Solomon said that you should listen to the sage advice and experienced wisdom of a learned teacher. I say, become a lifelong learner of relationships from those who give wise advice. He said that their advice will teach you how to think and speak. I say if you are not thinking about what you are thinking about so that you can speak the right things, you are wasting valuable time. He said that the words spoken by a loose (temporary) woman is sweet and smooth. I say that you should refrain from listening to someone who breaks up good relationships and begin listening to those who build them.

Solomon also said that she will bring you to bitterness. She will make you regret your life, is what I say. He said that men should stay away from ladies of that caliber before she takes them to Hades, the place of the dead. I say run as fast as, well, you know, away from her. He said that she will bring you shame, deception, weakness, poverty, groaning, mourning, and death. I say keep running as fast as you can while doing the daily disciplines that nurture the caliber of a champion. He said a lack of discipline and learning will kill you. I agree wholeheartedly because to be ignorant and undisciplined is akin to being a complete failure in life.

In Proverbs 5:15-19 Solomon gives instruction to men on how to love a permanent. You should take heed. Solomon advises that you *drink* from your own well (your wife) and let your children be born and raised by you and not another. That is how a permanent man operates, he confines himself to his own wife and runs his home well. She has his children and she has his heart. No games, no messing around and no temporaries. He enjoys his wife's body and is satisfied with delight in her love and with her love.

The Agaphilerosas and the Temporary

Agaphilerosas, (women who practice agaphileros), you pay so much for bad choices. Isn't it time that you got a break? Don't you want to be the one walking along the beach with someone who will love you for your lifetime? Don't you wish that you had understood then what you understand now? After you grew up a bit in relationships, you did the work, made the sacrifices and initiated the changes to become better, yet, another temporary. What is going on?

The answer to this may lie in a scripture in the Book of 1 Timothy 2:14 that says, **"And it was not Adam who was deceived, but [the] woman who was deceived and deluded and fell into transgression." [Gen. 3:1-6.]** This may be the single most important verse in the Love Manual for a woman who is considering getting involved with a man. Forget about Adam and his awful decision, if you can. This one's for you.

Eve was deceived. She allowed a thought that stimulated a passion she should have left alone. Ladies, when you think back on your past failed relationships, do you see any similarities between what Eve did and what you did? Eve allowed a temporary to come in and ruin a permanent thing. He tricked her and she lost her way. That man that treated you like dirt was a temporary and you just could not see it. You gave him permanent things, hoping that he did deserve it.

What is unusual about this is that God has blessed you with the ability to discern people and things, yet you have fallen for deception over and over again. Some call it a sixth sense that you possess. Satanas (Satan's Greek name), has been using the same strategy against you that worked on Eve. He wants to devalue you by deceiving you. If he can get you to think less of yourself, you will begin to think more of temporaries. You birth nations so if he can mess you up, he can affect nations. So satanas is definitely a culprit in the failure of your relationships.

But let us not leave all the blame at his feet. The Book of 1 John 3:7 also lets us know that people can deceive us. **"...let no one deceive you..."** (Amplified Bible, 1987). So, to continue the blame game, we see that people, and in your case, men, practice deception. Ultimately, all deception is rooted in the lies of satanas, but there are people who are willing to be used as tools of deception. Unfortunately for you, they are really good at fooling you and have perfected ways to get through the defenses of your sixth sense.

But there is one more scripture that reveals to us the last culprit in the CSI drama of deception. The Book of 1 Corinthians 3:18 says, **"Let no person deceive himself"** (Amplified Bible, 1987). Sorry to be the bearer of the bad news, but *you* are the final guilty party in this trilogy. The good news is that now that you know you are also to blame, you can do something about it. For whatever reason you chose to become self-deceived, today is a good day to stop and move in the opposite direction. Truth is your way out of temporaries *and* your way in to the path of a permanent lover.

Note that truth is not a doctrine, truth is a person; Jesus. He is the Way, the Truth and the Life. Truth and grace came through Him. Let me also add, a good permanent man will come through Him also. If you want a thing, why not go straight to the source to get it? He is the source of what you truly need; a permanent.

Permanents will get you to your destination. There is just something about them and your purpose in life. They fit right in. They will always point you in the direction of success and purpose. A permanent will play a large part in getting you to your *California*. It is conceivable that you will meet many temporaries along the way to your destiny. Some may be from your *Georgia* and may decide to travel with you. However, they may only go as far as *Alabama.* A person whose goal is *Alabama* is not your mate. Even if someone says that they will go with you until you get to *Texas.* They are not your mate. You need someone who is willing to go to the same destination as yourself. Don't be so head over heels that you forget to do your due diligence. Ask questions, often, and ask 1000 questions if necessary.

Find what permanent is for you and then pursue it, because if you do not know what permanent is then you may not know when temporary shows up. The most common relationship error today is people taking temporary things and trying to fit them into permanent positions. You are better than that.

Ladies, do not let the pain of the past keep you from the promise of the future. This was what God was telling me 10 months after my darling Jessy had passed. He said, "If you don't let go of the past, then I will not be able to give you the future that I have for you. Don't focus on her death. Focus on her life and the love that you both shared. Now go teach others." Hence Agaphileros.

Do not let a temporary keep you stuck in your past. No matter what they have done to you or taken from you, the permanent in your future will give you more than you ever thought possible. Focus on the good that has been prepared for you. Focus on the best that is coming your way. Focus on developing yourself, all 3 parts of yourself: spirit being, psychological being and physical being. Focus on being ready to handle someone that is beyond awesome.

How does a Permanent refine their character?

In order to be a permanent you must become a refiner

of character. Let me explain. Refinements are recalculations toward being a better person than you were before. A lack of refinement is a miscalculation toward being a worse person than you were before. Small miscalculations may have minimum impact like at a shooting range. But small miscalculations on a spacecraft heading out into space can have a major impact. You may end up way off course in a short amount of time.

If you never recalculate your life as a temporary it is very unlikely that you will ever really become a permanent because it takes work, requires sacrifice and demands change in order to become and remain a permanent. Do nothing and you will remain the way you are; a temporary. Work, sacrifice and change and you can become anything that you wish to be. Recalculate your life and you will engage the process of becoming a permanent.

How can you refine your character? Let us look at it from the angle of a river. The Book of Proverbs 4:23 says, **"Keep and guard your heart with all vigilance and above all that you guard, for out of it flow the springs of life"** (Amplified Bible, 1987). So we can see that whether you are a temporary or a permanent, what you are comes out of your heart. What have you deposited into your heart lately? Or better said, what have you allowed to be deposited into your heart? Yes beloved, you are the gate keeper of your heart and the one responsible for what is in your life.

What you let in determines the life you will have. So it sounds like a simple fix, doesn't it? Let in only what you want to see in your life and you will *see* what you let in. If you see something in your life that you do not like then it behooves you to check your filters. Something is getting in that is not beneficial to you, so you must address it.

I like the idea of a river because a river takes whatever you put in there and carries it to the ocean. That is your life. What you take in will ultimately be seen in the ocean of your life. If something negative and destructive has entered your river, do not wait until it gets to the ocean to fish it out. No beloved. When you notice it the first time, deal with it.

Beyond that, you and I are admonished to guard it. That is a military term. Do you want to be a permanent for someone? Then you have to possess a military mentality about protecting what enters your river or your heart because if it stays in your heart it will be in your life. Permanents are always on guard against temporary relationship thoughts.

Beloved, above all that you guard you must guard your heart. Most rivers are small and negotiable. Most oceans are vast and uncontainable. Having the discipline of a permanent is necessary for refinements to take place. If you do the daily assessments that can identify the things that you need to change, and then are able to address them on an immediate basis, you will be way ahead of the rest of the population in regards to being prepared for marriage.

On that note, let me reiterate something that I have said prior. I see relationships as entity themselves, and as you have to guard your own heart like a soldier, so too, the both of you should guard the heart of the relationship like soldiers. If there is some behavior that is detrimental to the relationship and it enters the river, right then and there is the time to deal with it.

Usually, when something enters a river it enters from the side where the currents are not too strong and the depth is pretty shallow. Given time, this item can meander to the middle of the river where it will be caught up in the stronger currents and the highest speed of the river. The longer you let a problem fester the greater the possibility that it will be a part of the ocean of your relationship.

As for the relationship, so for the individual. Permanents are not fearful of refinement. Refine your character daily so that you are not spending the bulk of your time trying to fish out things that should have been taken out a long time ago. Refine your behavior now so that you are not lost in a quagmire of debris that can damage your navigational systems. Refine your thinking today so that you do not end up like the Titanic and get gashed wide open by something you could have easily avoided.

How does a Permanent think?

Another way to refine your character is by refining the way you think. Many people fail in life because they first fail in mind. A great passage from the Love Manual that addresses the way we should think is from the Book of Romans 12:2. **"Do not be conformed to this world (this age), [fashioned after and adapted to its external, superficial customs], but be transformed (changed) by the [entire] renewal of your mind [by its new ideals and its new attitude], so that you may prove [for yourselves] what is the good and acceptable and perfect will of God, even the thing which is good and acceptable and perfect [in His sight for you]"** (Amplified Bible, 1987).

Your mind is like the tributaries and springs that feed your river or your heart. Paul is suggesting that as a person of faith you should be mentally transformed entirely and not partially. This new way of thinking is too important to stop before becoming 100% changed. Why? The will of God is at stake. Being transformed into a permanent has been a part of God's design for you from the beginning and you have to begin to think along those lines. It is God's will for you.

I have met a few people who did not believe that God could even give to them a love of a lifetime. Some doubted that permanents even existed today, and to be honest with you, if you spend your time allowing the national television networks and the social media gangs to infiltrate your tributaries, you will also think like that. Thank God for those who decided to put up a new filter and focus on what the Love Manual has to say about what God has for them.

Your character can change with a new approach to thinking but only in tandem with new things to think about. The change comes by renewal. It comes by deconstructing the false doctrines of love that exist in the world and constructing love the way it is supposed to be. It comes by deliberately spending more time in the Love Manual than in the porn manual. It comes by digging into the Love Manual and not digging into deviant behavior. It comes by constantly saying yes to permanent things and no to temporary things.

How does a Permanent build?

Permanents guard their hearts and think differently in order to be great builders. And might I add, when two permanents build a relationship it is a beautiful thing. However, you cannot build something that will last a lifetime with something designed for a short time. That is counterproductive. Permanent things + temporary things = weak relationship. Instead, find the materials that can serve you best and build with those instead. The fruit of the Spirit are great building materials: love, joy, peace, patience, gentleness, goodness, faithfulness, humility and self-control. No one can bring a charge against these materials. In other words, no devil in hell or person on earth can destroy a relationship built with permanent materials.

Finding a permanent is rare, but not impossible, and they are worth building with. God specializes in the impossible. Some people become frustrated and settle for less than the best because they have been with so many temporaries. Do not give up on meeting and building with a permanent.

Becoming a permanent is relatively easy also, when you do the right things to become one. However, as Jim Rohn often said what is easy to do, is also easy not to do. A spouse may decide at any time to become a permanent after years of being a temporary. Great! Support their transition. You cannot imagine how wonderful a permanent is until you have experienced one. And the build? It will be out of this world.

Trust me.

Ladies, let God refine you so your Boaz can find you. Simple refinements can lead to major attractions. Brothers, it is the small refinements that bring the greatest enjoyments. If you want to change something big, start with a small change. Break up the entire project into digestible pieces. If you want to remodel your house on your own, start with a door. When you are finished with the door it will become a reminder that the process has begun. Every time you walk through that door it will remind you to keep remodeling. Don't stand at the door, move on. Who's got next?

Beloved, a permanent is worth the wait, worth the cost and worth the effort. Those who build well usually finish well. A permanent will be with you through the toughest of times and through your most amazing of days. A relationship built by two permanents will set the stage for those who will come behind them to see what must be done in order to make relationships work.

Permanents, I believe in you, God believes in you, your spouse (present or future) believes in you and together you two will be the pillars upon which your family can stand strong for a lifetime. I salute you and wish you well (with your permanent self).

Take Aways M2

- ✓ A permanent person is someone who God brings into your life that He has specifically chosen for you so that you can enjoy the love of a lifetime. In that case, a *temporary* is someone who is *not* that person.

- ✓ *Never give up a permanent person for a temporary person.* This is a common mistake made by people who are immature and unstable in relationships. If you walk out on a permanent person you walk out on the best thing that could ever happen to you.

- ✓ *Never hook up to a temporary while waiting for a permanent to show up.* Do not become unequally yoked together with a temporary if you are a permanent waiting on a permanent.

- ✓ *Never try to hold permanent conversations with temporary-minded people.* Conversations by a permanent with a temporary will eventually become the equivalent of speaking to a brick wall. So in order to keep from pulling out your hair and having to invest in a weave, a toupee or a helmet, reserve permanent conversations for permanent people.

- ✓ All permanents recognize the power of words. They do not just speak words, they covenant. Every word out of the mouth of a permanent person is covenant based and love infused.

- ✓ *Never build anything permanent with a temporary person.* Many women, especially, have fallen for the smooth talking temporaries who eventually left them with the baby, the bills and the blame. Seems like he just said hello the other day and now it's all about the goodbye.

- ✓ Permanents focus on building things that last, whereas temporaries focus on building things fast.

- ✓ A temporary clothed in permanent clothing is a dangerous person, especially if you have built anything with them. They can become your worst nightmare. If the person in your life is not taking authority over their behavior to improve themselves, chances are that you may be dealing with a temporary in permanent clothing.

- ✓ When you say yes to who is temporary, you say no to who is permanent.

- ✓ Solomon said that the words spoken by a loose (temporary) woman is sweet and smooth. I say that you should refrain from listening to someone who breaks up good relationships and begin listening to those who build them.

- ✓ That is how a permanent man operates, he confines himself to his own wife and runs his home well. She has his children and she has his heart. No games, no messing around and no temporaries. He enjoys his wife's body and is satisfied with delight in her love and with her love.

- ✓ Eve was deceived. She allowed a thought that stimulated a passion she should have left alone. Eve allowed a temporary to come in and ruin a permanent thing.

- ✓ He wants to devalue you by deceiving you. If he can get you to think less of yourself, you will begin to think more of temporaries.

- ✓ Ultimately, all deception is rooted in the lies of satanas, but there are people who are willing to be used as tools of deception.

- ✓ *You* are the final guilty party in this trilogy. Today is a good day to stop and move in the opposite direction of deception. Truth is your way out of temporaries *and* your way in to the path of a permanent lover.

- ✓ Permanents will get you to your destination. There is just something about them and your purpose in life. They fit right in. They will always point you in the direction of success and purpose.

- ✓ Find what permanent is for you and then pursue it, because if you do not know what permanent is then you may not know when temporary shows up. The most common relationship error today is people taking temporary things and trying to fit them into permanent positions.

- ✓ In order to be a permanent you must become a refiner of character. Refinements are recalculations toward being a better person than you were before. A lack of refinement is a miscalculation toward being a worse person than you were before.

- ✓ I like the idea of a river because a river takes whatever you put in there and carries it to the ocean. That is your life. What you take in will ultimately be seen in the ocean of your life.

- ✓ Permanents are always on guard against temporary relationship thoughts.

- ✓ The longer you let a problem fester the greater the possibility that it will be a part of the ocean of your relationship.

- ✓ Another way to refine your character is by refining the way you think. Many people fail in life because they first fail in mind.

- ✓ You cannot build something that will last a lifetime with something designed for a short time. That is counter-productive. Permanent things + temporary things = weak relationship.

- ✓ Ladies, let God refine you so your Boaz can find you. Brothers, it is the small refinements that bring the greatest enjoyments. If you want to change something big, start with a small change.

MOVEMENT 3

New Wine in old Wineskins?

Do not sacrifice the beauty of your future by holding on to the bitterness of your past. It is over and they are not coming back. Move on and become new wine.

It's all about Relationships

Luke 5:36-39 (NKJV). **Then he spoke a parable to them: "No one puts a piece from a new garment on an old one; otherwise the new makes a tear, and also the piece that was taken out of the new does not match the old. And no one puts new wine into old wineskins; or else the new wine will burst the wineskins and be spilled, and the wineskins will be ruined. But new wine must be put into new wineskins, and both are preserved. And no one, having drunk old wine, immediately desires new; for he says, 'The old is better.' "**

This particular Movement is going to give you yet another way of looking at your relationship(s), especially eros relationships, so that you can get some understanding through revelation. Rabbi Jesus (His teaching title) actually taught more on relationships than on any other topic in the New Testament.

As a matter of fact, the Bible as a whole teaches more about relationships than anything else because we are always relating. We relate to God, to ourselves, to other people and to our environment all the time. Jesus taught on money, marriage, ministry, etc., and each lesson was about a relationship you have with those aforementioned things. Genesis to Revelation is all about relationships: who, why, how, when, where and what. When I read the Love Manual today, this is how I see it: as the premier book on relationships by the premier creator of relationships, the Lord God Almighty.

Jesus is the Wedge

According to this account by Luke, Jesus had recently called 2 types of disciples, overloaded 2 ships with a fish harvest, performed 2 types of healings, was confronted by 2 types of haters 2 times (scribes and Pharisees) and was questioned about 2 things that His disciples were doing. Jesus answered with a double parable (2) and compares the old with the new. Now what I am about to say may be slightly controversial but hear me through to the end.

Jesus Himself was and is God's wedge for time and in time. He is the *after* for your *before.* Wherever He showed up He brought people into a new relationship with God and did so deliberately at the expense of the old relationship they were involved in. He is still doing so today. Our own calendars say that we live in 2015 A.D. (the year of our Lord or Anno Domini). We have before Christ (B.C.) and after Christ (A.D.). Is it any wonder that you can find Jesus being the wedge wherever He goes? He is like the ultimate double edged sword. This propensity for separating or dividing is recorded at least three times in the Gospels; Matthew 10:35, Luke 2:34 and Luke 12:49-53.

Dictionary.com says that a wedge is a piece of hard

material with two principal faces that meet in a sharp acute angle and that it splits objects by the application of a driving force. Jesus has come to set people free from what holds them back from the best possible relationships that they could ever have. In this passage He is teaching about the old and the new, the past and the future. The scribes, the Pharisees and many of the law keepers wanted things to remain the same but Jesus brought a new way of relating to the entire world.

Many of us have experienced heartaches and heartbreaks on the paths of pleasure and pain. This may be where you are now. You have lived in average for a long time yet embedded in your soul is a sliver of hope that keeps telling you that you can have a better life. This cannot be all that God has for you. Surely a loving God can bring true and lasting love into your world. Beloved, He will, and He will use the Rabbi to move you from the old into the new, from the past into the future. Keep hope alive, keep believing and keep reading.

The Old versus the New

In keeping with the double theme, when He talks about the new garments and the new wine, He is talking about us and the relationships that we have had in the past versus the new relationship that He has brought us into. In this relationship parable you are the piece from the new garment and the new wine.

An old garment is just that; old. Have you ever picked up an old piece of cloth and it tore apart at will? Do you think that putting it through a sewing process will cause it to be better? Do you think that it can withstand a sewing machine? No beloved. It has served its purpose, it has run its course and it has finished its race. Now it is time for it to become a cleaning cloth, recyclable material or trash. The same is true for old wineskins. They are just like the old garments. They have served their original purpose and will not be able to effectively perform a new assignment with the old strategies and strengths.

And as goes old wineskins so goes your old relationships. Some were good, some were bad and some were ugly, but one thing for sure, they are over and done with. But are they? Did you really discard the cloth and toss the wineskin? If we checked in the closet of your heart will we see the old boyfriend, husband, girlfriend or wife still hiding in there? Selah.

Even for me who had an amazing marriage and an equally amazing wife, would it make sense to bring my next wife into a state of comparison to Jessy? Should I treat her just the same as I did Jessy? Should I strive to make my next marriage exactly like my old marriage? As much as I loved Jessy and as much as the Holy Spirit taught me through her, it would be unwise and anti-love to make her a measuring stick for some other wife or to make our relationship the end all for my next marriage.

Surely we had some great wine, the best I ever tasted and our relationship was a great wineskin, suited just right for the both of us, and yes, we were settling in for the long haul. Our wine was tasty and precious but our wine was poured out as an offering for Agaphileros. Do you understand? I did not fully comprehend what our purpose was back then but now I know. I would not be able to teach about relationships as I do now without having the experiences that I had then.

Have you ever done one of those *connect the dots* puzzles? Sometimes you cannot see the whole picture until you get close to the end and sometimes you see it *at* the end. This is where I am in terms of my purpose, I can see more clearly what I am supposed to do and who I must become in order to do so. Yet I must also prepare my wine for my next wife and she must prepare her wine for me. When we come together we must combine our wines into a new wineskin. Then and only then can we be properly sustained in the future that God is giving to us; a Championship Relationship.

Stretching your Skin

Let us speak some more about the parable and why some may not have understood its meaning or its implication. Maybe some readers could not grasp the parable that Jesus gave because this is foreign to their culture, but for those who were listening, they understood what He was talking about. I read an article from Dr. Ralph F. Wilson recently and learned some interesting things about wine and wineskins from that era. (I encourage you to Google all of this and dig deeper into the information).

Part of the fermentation process for the wine included storing it in the wineskin for a period of time. The wineskin of that day was usually a whole goat that was gutted with the head and the feet removed and the feet ports tied off. At a certain stage of the process the wine was placed into this wineskin and the head was then tied off. The carbon dioxide gas would cause a tremendous swelling to take place and the skin would be stretched to its limit. According to Dr. Wilson, at this point, "...the collagen protein that gives the leather its stretching ability has been stretched out," (Wilson, 2014).

He further states that at that point the skin's ability to contract and stretch again was gone. Did you catch that? I see old relationships just like that. Whether they were good, bad or ugly, they have run their course. Use them as references yes, but as containers for the new, definitely not. Trying to fit your new relationship into something that cannot contain its expansion will inevitably lead to both of you and the relationship falling apart.

Let me add some balance and clarification here. All past relationships have lessons to be learned. Everything affects something and all things can teach something to someone. A good relationship that is over has good memories and important mementos. It may also have kids, property, in-laws and other things that accompany the parties involved into the future. It may have ended because of death or divorce. Where Jessy was concerned I had to face death. I did have a memorial set up during my grieving process but after a while I had to move forward. I packed up the memorial and made some major changes in the house.

Eventually, I will relocate to another home but for now (as of the writing of this book) I am good where I am. She is at peace and so am I. I am now n*ew wine*. When my next wife comes along she will not have to do battle with an old relationship. I am better because of the old relationship but I am not stuck in its memories or mementos.

Others have had bad and ugly relationships and they have become bitter because of them. Know that the collagen for the bad and ugly relationships has been used up. Therefore, do not sacrifice the beauty of your future by holding on to the bitterness of your past. It is over. They are not coming back. Move on and become new wine.

Has anyone seen my Collagen?

Every relationship comes with its own level of collagen protein. Every relationship can only be stretched but so far. Every person in every relationship has to build and grow the relationship into something new. My advice, do not take your new girlfriend to your ex-girlfriend's favorite restaurant. Do not talk to your new boyfriend about the things that your ex-boyfriend used to do that made you feel like you were a queen. Do not spend too much time talking about the old wine and the old wineskin.

Your new wineskin can only bear but so much of that before it begins to leak and eventually break open. You have to realize that the other person is gone and the person in front of you needs your new wine as much as you need theirs. Develop new things together. There is a protein for that.

If you find that you have been in and out of many

relationships, check to make sure that you have not been trying to put the new relationships into the same old wineskin from the past. If you are in a relationship now that you are struggling in, check yourself. You may need to ask God to add some protein to it so that it can expand a bit. Sometimes, it may be the person on the other end of the line that has protein problems.

For example, if your new "friend" is constantly comparing you to their "ex-friend", now would be a good time to bury that old wineskin once and for all. Ask them to read this Movement (chapter) after you are finished reading it yourself. It can work if you both want it to work. You can get the job done if you solicit the help of the protein provider (God). You can survive and thrive. There is a protein for that.

I can *hear* you thinking about previous relationships and trying to see if you or the other person made those mistakes. Trust me, I know. I often analyze and over analyze things like old relationships just to see what I could have done better. My analyzing has always been sincere even when appearing sinuous or indirect. I want to make sure that I provide my next wife with the best husband that she could ever have. I am sure that you want to be the best spouse for your mate as well, even if you are already married. We can and we will be great spouses. There is a protein for that.

There is another perspective on wineskins that you must see and it is this. Some people have wineskins that *they* have created over time. They have the formula down pact: relationship + my level of protein = **my type of relationship**. They were hurt in the past so now they know what they want and do not want. This is a built in safety mechanism because past hurt makes you protect yourself in the future and rightly so.

However, I have seen it taken to the extreme, hence the formula above. Let me ask you a question. When God created the goat, did He ask *you* how much collagen protein needed to be in the goat's skin for it to be a good wineskin?

Do *you* know how much your relationship will have to stretch for you to have a Championship Relationship in the future? My suggestion to you is to stop making wineskins with your formula that God did not design or orchestrate.

In other words, stop mass producing these wineskins and placing every relationship into what you have created as if you know what it will need in the future. God is the only one who knows how much elasticity will be needed for your relationships and He adds just enough collagen protein to your relationships to make it last until the end. You have to believe that to receive it. God-ordained relationships have just enough protein for their survival, even unto the end.

Only God knew how much Jessy and I would have to face as a couple and how much we would have to stretch in order to make it to the end. There was enough collagen to last to the final breath of the relationship. I know for a fact that God brought us together. I know for a fact that He knew what was coming. I know for a fact that Agaphileros was to be born into the earth. And I know for a fact that He gave us just enough protein to keep us together until her final breath.

Beloved, your collagen level is enough for anything that will come against your relationship or anything that will try to pull it apart. Your elasticity will be enough. He designed it so. Just be sure that you are not manufacturing failure by self manufacturing the protein needed for your relationship.

The Truth about Protein

A little scientific side bar for the moment. Protein itself can come in many forms other than collagen. For example, our bodies contain hemoglobin that is used for our internal transport system. Don't you know that your relationship needs some hemoglobin as well? Your relationship is a ship, designed by God to go somewhere, especially when that relationship is marriage. Adam said that a man should leave his father and mother and cleave to his wife, where the 2 then become 1. There is movement in a marriage and that is why you need God to put the right protein in it for you.

Another protein that our bodies use is called antibodies and these assist in the body's defense mechanisms, specifically the immune defense system. Your relationship has to be defended against all fear, terror and enemies; foreign and domestic. The defense protein is designed to protect you from your enemies. Your spouse is not your enemy.

Enzymes are another important protein for our bodies. They help to provide the metabolism that we need to function day in and day out. Enzymes help to produce, maintain and destroy an organism's material substance. To produce certain structures (good traits and habits) in your relationships you will need protein. To maintain what is produced will require even more protein.

Finally, to destroy what needs destroying (negative traits and habits) in your relationship you will also need protein. In all of this, energy is needed in order to accomplish the purpose for your relationship. Your body can use protein to provide both energy for purpose and energy to destroy as well. Oh, and by the way, stop the "friendly fire" so common between couples. Your spouse is supposed to be your friend.

Beloved, I think that I am talking to all of us at this point. We all fall short sometimes but that does not mean that we should want to keep falling short. So often we had the right person but used the wrong skin. We let them go or chased them away. We tried to fit them into an old way of thinking and relating that only suited our plans and not theirs until there was no room for them? It is never about one person, it is always about both people and the purpose for the relationship.

Maybe they did not fit our criteria for what wine should look like and taste like. Unfortunately, we can become like wine tasters or wine connoisseurs just spitting people out because we do not like their flavor. Beloved, God knows best, not you. I urge you to trust Him for the right type and level of protein for your marriage and relationships.

Sweet Tooth

Notice the 3 things that Jesus said that "no one" does: **no one** puts a new piece of cloth on an old garment, **no one** pours new wine into old wineskin, and **no one** drinks old wine and say that they immediately want new wine. The Rabbi said the same thing in 3 different ways. Again I have to thank Dr. Ralph F. Wilson for his research of the text.

The reason that a person would prefer the old over the new is because the old is sweet and ready for consumption. The reason that the new is not welcome is because it is not yet smooth and finely aged as the old. He said of the new wine, "It may be a bit sharp and unrefined. But it is alive. You can't contain it in old structures. You must find new wineskins for it or none at all." (Wilson, 2014). The old and the new cannot mingle together. They are like oil and water; they will not mix properly.

If you had a good relationship in the past, do not expect that your new relationship will automatically be as sweet. The new relationship has to go through its fermenting stages. Give the relationship time to expand. Sometimes a good *early relationship disagreement* serves to reveal just how much you may need to expand later on to keep the relationship going. No worries though. Keep expanding.

If God is in it, give it a chance to mature. I have seen today how easy it is to break up with someone even if God brought you both together. People are more impatient than ever before. We want what we want and we want it yesterday. You cannot get a good relationship going and growing by jumping in when it feels good and jumping out when it stretches you. We all need stretching. It is a part of being a champion. Before every activity the champion athlete engages in at least one thing; stretching. Why?

One reason is that it gets the muscles ready for

pressure. Another reason is that it keeps the body from getting hurt. Also, stretching can maximize muscle potential. Stretching is essential. God has provided your relationship with enough elasticity for your maturity. Relationship maturity is confirmed at the end of your stretching and not at the beginning so please hold your applause until maturity is confirmed.

I have had to make several self-adjustments since Jessy died. I once heard that the men that landed on the moon took several days and made about 10 trajectory adjustments before they could get there. If they were strong headed they would have ventured into space never to be heard from again. Do not become so stubborn that you are unwilling to make adjustments. Trust the God of the wineskin. The God who invented relationships must surely know how to stretch you into a good one.

Another thing that I will add to your knowledge base is this. Please do not throw an ex's name or deeds into the face of your current lover during a heated discussion. It may cause some irreparable damage to your wineskin. Save the drama 4 yo mama.

Beloved, let me interject a word of the Lord to those of you that have been through a great relationship that blessed you beyond your wildest dreams. It is over and they are gone. Maybe it ended unexpectedly or you had some great years then it fell apart. However it ended you should know this, as good as it was, is not as good as it gets. What God has prepared for you is so vast and beyond what you have ever experienced that if you could see the future you would refrain from worrying and complaining about it. It may have been good but God has an even better one coming to usher you into your Championship. Read the story of Boaz and Ruth from the Love Manual and see how they exemplify this.

Let me mention one more thing about old sweet wineskins. Even if you revisit an old lover there is no guarantee that what you had will work again. No matter how good it was, things change and people change. Many factors may have taken root in both your lives and now you are not the same people. Changes may have come in the areas of mindsets, attitudes, family, in-laws, geography, priorities, purpose, focus and the list goes on and on. I knew a soul who once visited an old friend with whom they hoped to refill the old wineskin but alas, no more collagen. The protein was all gone. So the wineskin busted open and they both fell out.

That which was old felt good to them and was comfortable as well. That was the "wisha coulda shoulda" syndrome. They came away from that wineskin with a valuable lesson: trying to rekindle something that is old may not always work. It might, with the right conditions, but more often than not, the wine will not even look or taste the same as before. Beloved, new wine that has been properly fermented and aged brings with it tantalizing stimulations for the physical and psychological nature that can make even the most experienced relationship sommelier blush with delight. As long as the new is given a chance to be processed and allowed to become mature, it will eventually be tastier than any wine that you have ever tasted.

So the next time you have a glass of wine, think about how much it had to go through in order to arrive in your glass. Also, the next time you see an older couple holding hands or holding each other or just loving on each other, realize that the wineskin you see is not an overnight package or a temporary pleasure. They did not get there by jumping in and out of relationships. They decided to do the work, make the sacrifices and initiate the necessary changes along the way. New wine can become sweet wine.

Ready, Set, Process

Dr. Wilson also lets us know the stages of the process: "the crushing of the grapes, the first state of fermentation, the straining and separating, then finally into the new wineskin"

(Wilson, 2014). Some of us rush the process of getting married or getting into a serious relationship before we have gone through the process of being made ready. Some of us also get involved with people that are still grapes; they have not been crushed yet. How would you know what is within a person if they have never been through anything?

Allow them to stretch a little on their own first before stretching together with them. Make sure that they have been strained and separated from certain things before getting into that new wineskin with them. But once you both are no longer grapes and are ready to grow together, go for it.

Practice makes Perfect Protein

Let us now apply some practical things that you can do to have that new wineskin and enjoy its sweetness.

Step A. *Learn to let go of the past spiritually so that you can attend to the future that God has for you. Your best is not in your past, it is in your future.*

1. Begin to believe that God has created a future for you. Jeremiah 29:11.

2. Begin to believe that God can take the good, the bad and the ugly and make it work out in your favor. Romans 8:28.

3. Begin to make every step a step of faith in grace and mercy. Ruth 2:1-3.

Step B. *On purpose release the old garments (sheets), the old wine skins (relationships) and the old wine (all the exes) from your psychological being.*

1. Renew your mind to it. Romans 12:1-2.

2. Release them from your soul with self-talk including the words of forgiveness. If they treated you badly then you were the best thing they never had. Matthew 18:21-22

3. Remember the value of NEXT! If they are gone then it is very unlikely that they are ever coming back. Be like the Michelin Man and smile because the next one is coming. 1 Corinthians 7:10-15

Step C. *What can you physically do right now to prepare for your new wine skin?*

1. Clear your line of sight. I had to pack up my memorial to Jessy after my grieving process because it would be unfair to bring someone else into her memory and mementos. Be respectful, but at the same time pace yourself forward. Ruth had to leave her family, her friends, her homeland, her husband's burial place, some of her stuff, and her old way of living in order to have a clear line of sight to see Boaz. You cannot find a good Boaz or a good Ruth with your line of sight all clogged up with old wine and wine skins.

2. Continue in good disciplines. If they have dropped off pick them up again. Ruth was not looking for a regular guy and Boaz was not looking for a regular damsel. They were both taking care of business, they were both in good disciplines. Are you in school? Study. Are you on a job? Do it well. Do you own a business? Run it properly. Ruth was working in the fields and out-working the young virgins who she met there. Get busy taking care of you with good rest, enough exercise and healthy eating habits.

3. Come boldly to the throne of grace. Hebrews 4:15-16. It is a throne of favor. We do not deserve it but God gives it to us anyway. That is grace. That was me with Jessy. For a while I stood in the shadows scared to approach her, but when I finally decided to man up, God's favor showed up. God's grace is sufficient for anything and everything.

A Whole New World

I used to think that when a man and a woman come together in a personal loving marital relationship they should *merge* their 2 worlds together. After further research and personal mistakes I now understand what Adam meant when he said that a man should leave his parents and cleave to his wife (Genesis 2:24-25). I now believe that it is best to *create* a new world, a future world where you both decide what enters and what does not. This allows you both to own the future and create the one that suits the both of you. Everyone and everything does not belong in your future and you have to be sensitive to the Holy Spirit to know the difference.

Now, I am not advocating spookiness and psychotic behavior where you stop talking to everyone and stop doing everything you were doing before you met. I am talking about 2 adults building a world where they both can be happy together with only what they desire invited inside. When God wanted a family He *created* a world. When Jessy and I became a married couple she told me that we were a brand new family. Our other "family members" became relatives in a sense but together she and I were *family;* 2 people who build a household under God. I knew what she meant. That was when we began to *create* our new world.

Beloved, as *you* develop into fine wine make sure and get all the extra stuff and extra people out of your wineskin before it is too late. Your collagen protein is only good for stretching two people. Let that be the both of you. Make sure there is a good straining/filtering process in your relationship. The period before the proposal is where you should discuss who and what is coming on your journey. Again, don't be weird but be wise. Don't be suspicious but be smart. Don't be an accuser but be an encourager. Build "a whole new world" like the song says and enjoy the process.

If you build it they will come

A great marriage is built just like a great championship team is built. Various parts make the whole and each player knows their role. A championship marriage can last a lifetime if you build it right. It took Jessy and I about 10 years to build a great friendship and out of that foundation we had about 16 years of a Championship Marriage. It was a great run yet it is now time for me to build another championship team because the first team has finished its course.

You may be facing a similar opportunity. Building and/or rebuilding requires many building blocks. Assessment, honesty and application are three of the building blocks needed. Assess the situation, be honest about what has to change then apply the change to the situation. Great teams never try to recapture the glory days because they are gone. What matters now is the future, not the past. The past is a reference point, a place and time to reminisce not to return. If you live to and for the past your life will be in reverse. You have to live for the future so that your life and all that is therein will move forward. You cannot change the past but your future will be changed by your decisions today.

As you rebuild, you must build on what was good and deal with what was "no good". If "no good" is allowed to enter the new team then it will cause the demise of the new team. No coach, manager or team owner wants to build on what was "no good"? They build on good things.

On a flight one day I was involved in a casual conversation with a lady. The one thing that she said that I wrote down was that you cannot put an old head on a young shoulder. She was referring to ideas and implementation. It was another way of saying what Jesus was saying in our text.

I submit this to you. Sometimes, one of the biggest relationship failures is trying to relive the past with a new person. Especially for us "old schoolers" that have been through a few relationships. We have to get delivered from an old way of thinking, an old way of processing and an old way of being. Everything else in this world strives for new and improved ways of doing things except for some of us old schoolers. We want something that looks like *this* when it is time to have something that looks like *that*. When you refuse to change from an old way of bad thinking good people may exit your life.

Personally, I have learned my lesson and I hope that you have as well. I am no longer trying to put new wine into old bottles. I am no longer trying to build new relationships upon old neck and shoulders. Beloved, let go of the past so that God can give you the future that He has for you. Let go of the old so that He can bring you the new. Go to the Love Manual and believe what you read. He has a new man or a new woman for you that will take you into the final frontier; agaphileros.

Stop depending on only what you know. Your knowledge is limited. Start depending on God and what He has planned for you. If your current relationship is leaking with issues right now then the plug may be right here: build it upon a new neck and shoulders, and build on previous good things.

We Can! You Can!

Being transparent is one of the tools that I use to teach others with. **We can** and should be transparent. Yes, **you can** too. People will be able to see the real you and trust what you say and do. I believe that people understand people that are real. I am not just a writer. Much of what I write now had to be experienced in order for me to get the depth of understanding that I have now. I have messed up many times and even now my pulse beats with imperfections.

I have experienced what I am sharing with you today. I have been the one who took the old wine into a new relationship and I have been the new wine being poured into an old relationship. Neither panned out and feelings were hurt; theirs and mine. Beloved, I reveal my life so that **we can** see what to do and what not to do. **We can** do it. **You can** do it.

Having a wife like Jessy taught me a lot about new wine and old wine skins. We had to obtain new wineskins to contain our new relationship. And I am sure that if she was here right now she would echo the sentiments that I share with you. I wish everyone would seek to understand relationships with a depth of desire that goes beyond just a passing inquiry. There are an abundant amount of anointed resources that are available today in order to do so.

We can stop the cycle of pain, hurt, abuse and failure that permeate our relationships today. **We can** drive down the negative rates of divorce, domestic violence, incest, child abuse, verbal abuse, physical abuse, psychological abuse, murders and wars. **We can** see more and more people that really do love others in a genuine way exhibiting this love through grace in action. **We can** if we do the work, make the sacrifices and initiate the changes necessary. Yes beloved, **you can** work, sacrifice and change.

Many people do not even survive the first real argument because they are weak in the areas of work, sacrifice and change. Know that you cannot go from weak to strong overnight. It takes time, resources and energy; it takes prayer, faith and believing; it takes commitment, persistence and tenacity; it takes openness, willingness and meekness.

To become a champion in your relationships is like being enrolled in a fitness facility. Attendance, training and passion will have to be a part of your life to become an avid fitness enthusiast. It is the same in relationships. Attend to your growth and development. Train on schedule until loving right becomes second nature, then eventually first nature. Be passionate about the people in your circle and especially about the person that you will be intimate with. Strong passions feed commitment which ultimately breeds better performance. **You can** do it.

Do not get caught up in the Hollywood hype, the tumultuous tabloids and the deceptive dramas that you are seeing daily. Relax yourself. Settle down. Be at peace. Wine matures better when it is at peace. Are you at peace? **You can** be. Are you aging better? **You can**. Or maybe you are concerned that you let a good person go and it still bothers you. No worries. God has many more good ones in the earth. Look for the new, but through the eyes of the Holy Spirit.

He may bring them to you looking less than perfect, but if *He* brings them, then there *is* potential (what can be) and there *will* be performance (changes for the better). Do not run away (fear) at the first few signs of minor challenges. No one is perfect all the time. Challenges will come and you will have to work (faith) through them. You both will be better people (sweet wine) because of it and it will bring you closer together (collagen).

Jessy and I were never closer than when she faced her medical challenges. Challenges are just opportunities to grow, to stretch and to become better. Her condition was an opportunity for us to stretch a little further than we had stretched before. Many times you will not know the depth of your love until a challenge shows up to do a depth check. How deep is your love? (Cue the Bee Gees).

If you run out of relationships whenever a challenge shows up, maybe your level of love is not as deep as you think. Get to the love gym because **you can** be better. New muscles will not show up in a day and neither will a better you.

Finally beloved, do not be too hard on yourself or be under conviction if you have messed up. We have all fallen short and the same grace that helped someone else rise like a phoenix will help you to rise up. The same Holy Spirit that comforted others during their toughest moments will comfort you. The same pressure that produced pain then gain will do the same for you. New wine does not age overnight.

This is what **you can** do and should do. Find an area of your life that you had to be stretched into previously and had a measure of success in the stretch. Maybe it was in some type of ministry or the military or health or education or parenting or business. Either way, since you have survived, use that memory as a springboard for an increased commitment to grow and become new like new wine. As you allow God to make you into a better wine, you will see your lover become an addicted loveraholic just for you. **You can** do it and beloved, you will! Drink up.

Take Aways M3

- ✓ The Bible as a whole teaches more about relationships than anything else because we are always *relating*; always.

- ✓ Jesus is God's wedge for time and in time. He is the *after* for your *before*.

- ✓ Jesus specifically came to set people free from what holds them back from the best possible relationships that they could ever have.

- ✓ Old cloths and old wineskins have run their course, they have finished their race, they have served their original purpose and will not be able to effectively perform a new assignment with the old strategies and strengths.

- ✓ Trying to fit your new relationship into something that cannot contain its expansion will inevitably lead to both of you and the relationship falling apart.

- ✓ Be better because of old relationships but do not get stuck in their memories or mementos.

- ✓ Do not sacrifice the beauty of your future by holding on to the bitterness of your past. It is over.

- ✓ You have to realize that the other person is gone and the person in front of you needs your new wine as much as you need theirs. Develop new things together. There is a protein for that.

- ✓ Stop making wineskins with your formula that God did not design or orchestrate.

- ✓ God ordained relationships have just enough protein for their survival, even unto the end.

- ✓ Godly protein can also help in the transportation system, defence mechanism and metabolism system of your relationship.

- ✓ A good relationship in the past does not mean that your new relationship will automatically be as sweet. The new relationship has to go through its fermenting stages. Give the relationship time to expand.

- ✓ Relationship maturity is confirmed at the end of your stretching and not at the beginning.

- ✓ Do not become so stubborn that you are unwilling to make adjustments.

- ✓ As good as it was for you is not as good as it will get for you. The best is on the way. Trust God.

- ✓ Some of us also get involved with people that are still grapes; they have not been crushed yet. How would you know what is within a person if they have never been through anything? Allow them to stretch a little on their own first before stretching together with them.

- ✓ You cannot find a good Boaz or a good Ruth with your line of sight all clogged up with old wine and wine skins.

- ✓ When you decide to man up, God's favour will show up.

- ✓ Create a new world, a future world where you both decide what enters and what does not.

- ✓ A great marriage is built just like a great championship team is built. Various parts make the whole and each player knows their role.

- ✓ Assessment, honesty and application are three of the building blocks needed for building a Championship Relationship. Assess the situation, be honest about what has to change then apply the change to the situation.

- ✓ The past is a reference point, a place and time to reminisce not to return.

- ✓ When you refuse to change from an old way of bad thinking good people may exit your life.

- ✓ We can and should be transparent. People believe and trust transparent people.

- ✓ You cannot go from weak to strong overnight. It takes time, resources and energy; it takes prayer, faith and believing; it takes commitment, persistence and tenacity; it takes openness, willingness and meekness.

- ✓ Strong passions feed commitment which ultimately breeds better performance.

- ✓ Wine matures better when it is at peace.

- ✓ Challenges are just opportunities to grow, to stretch and to become better.

MOVEMENT 4

The X Factor

We often gravitate to that which is cheap and available rather than what is precious and invisible.

What is the X Factor

The relationships that God has designed and assigned to your life are all going to end up being a blessing to you and not a curse. He is the designer of life and by default the Love Manual has been provided to help you to construct a life beyond limits. When considering getting into a relationship, I believe that we should trust the Designer. This is vitally important on many levels but one reason that stands out to me more than all others is the X Factor.

What is the X Factor you ask? It is the unknown part of a relationship, the future challenge that will shake you down to the very core of who you are if and when it comes. It waits in the uncharted season (that fifth season) like a sucker punch, it sits in the dark like an assassin and it is only known by God.

The Book of Job in the Love Manual is a good representation of the X Factor. Beloved, it can be the death of a child; the loss of all resources; it can be sickness in the body that strains your faith; it may be the spouse that refuses to grow in love anymore; it can often be the death of a loved one and things of that nature. It is that thing that you said will never happen. The X Factor for me was my Jessy going on to be with the Lord at 49 years of age. *"That will never happen to us, not until we are old and gray or Jesus returns."* That is what I said because that is what I believed.

There are many X Factors in the Love Manual as well. God put some people together and yet look at some of the things that occurred. Eve took the fruit and Adam ate it with her and it opened the door to sin and death to become active in the earth. Abraham tried to "help" God by having a baby with Hagar because the wife that God gave him was barren at the time. Division ensued within the family and Abraham had to send his first son away.

Rachel died in childbirth and she was the love of Jacob's life. He worked 14 years for her father just to obtain her hand in marriage. It cut him to the core. David used the Bathshebean Approach to take the mother of his God-ordained successor from her honorable husband. Mary became pregnant with Jesus without having sex with a man and Joseph her espoused husband had to deal with that situation. I guess we all are in good company because if they had to face X Factors and they survived then, we can also.

Some of you that are reading this portion of my assignment are thinking about the X Factor that came into your own life. You have been there and you have survived it. Yet, we also know of others that have not survived their X Factor. Why? It can be emotionally devastating and may cause some people to fall into depression, develop illnesses of their own, end up in financial ruin or grow a negative attitude. Unfortunately, some sufferers never recover to have successful relationships.

There are those who have decided that if loving someone causes that much pain, why love at all? They choose to live love free and in their minds they will remain pain free. The X Factor is no joking matter and if you are reading this but have never had something enter your life that can be called an X Factor, the time to prepare is now.

Being prepared is better than being surprised. If you know that it will rain will you not build a house with a roof and some walls to take shelter? Because most people consider themselves optimistic they go through life honky dory expecting only good to show up. Being optimistic is a good thing, but it is better to be a prepared optimist than an unprepared optimist when the X Factor arrives. Jessy and I had been prepared through our relationship with the Lord and our love for each other. We could not see the future but we had an unwavering trust in the one who held our future in his hands.

We did not know it then, but all the days of ministry in Carenage Pentecostal Church, my years at Ebenezer Temple and Bible Way Temple Church, followed by being members at World Changers Church International really solidified our relationship for what was about to come. Beloved, we do well to prepare for something that may never show up rather than to be unprepared for it when it does.

Only God knows the Big Picture

So often people only see the immediate benefits of a relationship without considering the full spectrum of what it may entail from start to finish, from the first hello to the final breath. Some people are convinced that they know exactly what to do in order to handle whatever will come their way. When things are going well their plan is working. They move God to the side because He is too old fashioned, yet they run to Him when their relationships face X Factors. There is hardly anything to bring you to a place of humility as much as an X Factor.

Allow me to paint the picture for you. Harry wants to be married. So does Jane. They have never met. They each have a certain list of conditions that they want in a spouse.

They have both been in failed relationships and so have been very disappointed before. They decide to protect themselves by "the list". The person they fall in love with has to be in the 95 percentile of the list, after all, we live in a modern technological world and we should always go with the numbers that work in our favor.

They finally meet one day. They seem to be a perfect fit. But Harry also has Pearl and Diamond in his life, two women that fit most of the criteria, but they do not meet as much of it like Jane does. After deciding that he has to focus on only one of them, Harry finally decides on Jane. After deciding to do that, he does what some people (author included) do, he takes his list and his choice to God. He informs God that he has found the perfect match and her name is Jane. He now wants God to bless who *he* has chosen and the relationship that they are creating.

However, as he spends time in prayer, the Holy Spirit begins to talk to him about Diamond. Harry lets the Holy Spirit know that in this modern day we live in that it would be best to go with the highest percentile. Chances are best with the highest percentile. He even produces data from the internet to support his position and has convinced himself that he has made the "best" choice. He has his mind and heart set on Jane.

Do you know why the Holy Spirit was talking to him about Diamond? It is because the Holy Spirit knows your future and he knows exactly who to place in your life so that he can maximize your purpose. He also knows that things will change after a while for Harry and he has equipped Diamond to help Harry to make it through successfully. There is an X Factor in his future and Diamond is his best option according to God's design.

Beloved, most people that have successful marriages do not have them by chance, they have them on purpose. You hardly ever stumble into a Championship Relationship. It usually takes a tremendous effort from both parties. Jane might look good for now but Diamond only needed some time to get to where she needed to be. Nevertheless, like Harry, most people decide on what they want, even when the Holy Spirit has placed red flags everywhere in your path. You have mucho banderas rojas yet you still head down the aisle (sometimes literally) or paths like the bulls of Pamplona. Are you aware of what happens to those bulls at the end of the day?

Not my will but Yours, Oh Lord

Jesus gives us the perfect example to making decisions while praying to the Father in the Garden of Gethsemane, "**… nevertheless not My will, but Yours, be done.**" (Matthew 26:39 NKJV). Do you not know that this is a perfect approach to take even *and* especially in developing relationships? The Holy Spirit knows exactly what your X Factor will look like. Trust Him. Even if you have a list, do not put your list ahead of God's will for your life. Maybe you will never experience an X Factor (and I pray that you will have a life without an X Factor), but God's will is still the best path to choose because of all the things that He has prepared for you.

Recently I began to pray certain words over my life and this is why. In October of 2012 the Lord spoke to me and one of the things that He mentioned was that He had a future prepared for me. So this list that I had for my second wife was eventually surrendered and now I pray to God that He will give to me the future that He has for me and not the one that I want to manufacture from my own efforts. This future includes a most beautiful, amazing and virtuous woman for me. Could she be reading this right now? I hope so.

Beloved, I am not advocating becoming a couch potato while God brings your spouse to your house. You still have to seek God about the other areas of your life and what is in store for you in the future. You still have to pray for your spouse before you meet them. You still have to live the zoe life right now. Your self-efforts can produce something, but I believe that your dependence on God will produce the best because God knows best.

When Jessy and I were thinking about being together, God chose to speak to both of us separately. That made it easier. I wish everyone that sought the Lord could get an answer as clear as we both received. Suffice it to say we knew God's choice. Even when I tried to deviate from it because of selfishness I ended up right back at the right choice at the right time. I did not have a list then and I did not know about any X Factors. All I knew was that this was the best that God had for me. Once I began to fall in line with His will, the relationship began to grow into a Championship Relationship.

Prepared for the X Factor

Beloved, let me tell you how God prepared me for the X Factor. One day while at work at the People's Bank in Hartford, Connecticut, I was sitting at the Customer Service counter thinking about Jessy. The Holy Spirit asked me a question very clearly. He asked me if I would still marry Jessy if she was disabled from a fire or accident. It seemed like a weird question yet I contemplated it for 2 weeks. After realizing the depth of my love for her I finally said that I would. A disabled Jessy was worth more to me than some other able bodied woman. I placed that kind of value upon her. What value have you placed on the person that you say that you love?

Not too long after that I was in Trinidad asking her to marry me. She said yes and I was batting 1000%. After years of bliss I had forgotten about that conversation with the Holy Spirit. What I did not know was that 16 years later we would enter into an uncharted season, one that birthed the X Factor of a lifetime. Do you think she could have handled all that she did with her own choice by her side? Do you think that I could have found a better person to serve God with? Do you believe that we were not meant to share the X Factor together? She indeed became a person with a physical disability but I was built for her disability. We made the right choice, the God choice. We were not perfect, but we were perfect for each other. We were stronger together; 1 chased 1000 but the right 2 chased 10,000.

   I do not wish an X Factor on anyone, but do you not think that you should go with the choice God has for you rather than the choice you make for yourself? I would not ever go with my own choice over God's choice. It is great when they are both the same but marriage is too important to be wrong. Let me say it this way. If your enemy can get you to mess up where your choice of a spouse is concerned he can wreak havoc into your purpose. Many people die every day with purposes unfulfilled because they hooked up with the wrong choice and when the X Factor showed up they could not handle it. Please do not be one of those people.

   I also felt led by the Holy Spirit to include the following 2 Movements on selecting a spouse to assist those who may be looking for their spouse. God will not choose for you someone who is bent on deviating from His word. God will not choose someone who wants to beat and abuse you. God will not choose for you a liar who destroys your trust. God will not choose one who will stress you into sickness and disease. God will not choose for you a person that relishes in the works of the devil, one who loves deception, darkness, deprivation, depravation, destruction and death. No sir, no ma'am, you will have someone of truth, born of the light, and filled with the zoe life of God. The X Factor is too major for God not to prepare the best for you. He will give you the best for the test. All that He has for you is the best.

   The best does not exclude storms and issues. It just means that you give yourself the best opportunity to come out on top as a couple. Storms are no respecter of relationships or marriages. Jesus talked about the storms that came into the lives of the one that followed His instruction and the one that did not. It was the same storm but it yielded different results (Matthew 7:24-29). The wise heard and followed through on what Jesus said but the foolish did not. The word used for "rain" denotes a violent rainstorm. Beloved, know that you need the Holy Spirit to talk to you because the X Factor can be like a violent storm, like a hurricane. Unless you are grounded into the right foundation your house/relationship will not pull through.

God is the key during the times of challenges, He makes your relationship strong, He makes your foundation firm and He guides you through the darkest of times. He is the threefold cord in the X Factor. A threefold wrapped cable is harder to break than a single string of cable. When both of you are joined together by God and your relationship is relying on God, you become a force for impact.

Please keep reading into the next 2 Movements as they are designed to stimulate thought and action. They are not self-help sections but rather self-less sections, a place where anyone can turn to in order to become better. People everywhere are choosing divorce over reconciliation, to quit rather than to change, to kill you rather than to keep you. So the next time you pull out your list of options that you want added to the menu, be careful, because Jane just might make your life a living hell. Harry too.

Take Aways M4

- ✓ What is the X Factor you ask? It is the unknown part of a relationship, the future challenge that will shake you down to the very core of who you are if and when it comes. It waits in the Uncharted Season (that fifth season) like a sucker punch, it sits in the dark like an assassin and it is only known by God.

- ✓ Some people have deduced that if loving someone can result in that much pain, why love at all? They choose to live love free and in their minds they will remain pain free.

- ✓ Being prepared is better than being surprised. Being optimistic is a good thing, but it is better to be a prepared optimist than an unprepared optimist when the X Factor arrives.

- ✓ We will do well to prepare for something that may never show up rather than to be unprepared for it when it does.

- ✓ So often people only see the immediate benefits of a relationship without considering the full spectrum of what it may entail from start to finish, from the first hello to the final breath.

- ✓ Beloved, most people that have successful marriages do not have them by chance; they have them on purpose. You hardly ever stumble into a Championship Relationship.

- ✓ Your self-efforts can produce something but I believe that your dependence on God will produce the best because God knows best.

- ✓ Do not ever go with your own choice over God's choice. It is great when they are both the same but marriage is too important to be wrong.

- ✓ God is the key during the times of challenges, He makes your relationship strong, He makes your foundation firm and He guides you through the darkest of times.

MOVEMENT 5
A word to the Agaphilerosa

If he is Mr. Right and he is doing the right things, then he will wait for what is rightfully his.

Mr. Right will love you right

Hello my sisters. This Movement is for your eyes. When Mr. Right comes along he will be willing to wait. If he is right then he can wait for what is right. Never be so desperate that you invite Mr. Wrong into a place that belongs to Mr. Right. Never be so pressured that you give your permanent things to some temporary guest that will leave you with endless stress. Never compromise what you possess to get a man that you cannot keep. Never trust a man who tells you that all his past relationships failed because of other people. Never fall for a pick up line that is designed to drag you down. Never sow your pearls before swine. Never settle for the bottom of the barrel when you were designed for the top. Never let your mouth take you where your body should not go. Never dress to attract lust, dress for love.

The Greek version of the word "husband" from the Love Manual said that a husband is how you distinguish an adult man from a boy. Never ask a boy to do a husband's job. Never trust a boy who cannot give you evidence of what he is saying. Never allow a boy to treat you like a piece of meat. Never honor boys who call you out of your name by giving them any of your time and attention. Never call yourself anything less than who you really are. You should never compromise, quit, cave in, or give up on being who you are supposed to be. Never.

Recently I saw a situation that has become more common today than it should be. While filling my gas tank at a gas station in Atlanta I observed a young lady pull up to another fuel pump. She exited her vehicle and I saw that there was a young man in the passenger seat. They both looked to be in their 20's. She began walking to the inside of the store to pay for the gasoline when he called out to her to get him some cigarettes. He then sat back and placed his sneaker wearing foot upon her dashboard. As she returned and gave him the cigarettes, she turned to pump the gasoline without being offered any help. I almost cried.

There is much that I can say about this scenario but what I want to say here is this. There are some things that he did *not* do which spoke volumes to me: He did not pay for the gasoline, he did not purchase the cigarettes he wanted, he did not offer to go into the store, he did not pump the gasoline, and he placed his dirty foot upon her dashboard. I am not sure why some women do not like to be nourished and cherished by the man that they are with. It befuddles me.

Now, I do not know all the particulars of their relationship so I speculate a bit here, but the obvious things are *obvious*. Question, are women really lowering their standard that much for a relationship? Are we as a nation giving up on good wholesome relationships between a man and a woman? Have we fallen so far that women allow men to treat them like they are worth nothing in public? And if this is public treatment what does private treatment look like? I know that not all men or relationships are like this, but I highlight the negative to show the need for more of the positive.

I can recall another incident that happened when I was giving out food samples at a store that I worked at in the past. A young couple walked up and I placed the first sample out. The man took it and opened his mouth wide to eat it at once. I was appalled. I remarked to him quickly, "Hey, aren't you going to give that to the lady first?" He froze in mid-air, mouth open, elbows bent, as his eyes moved to her face. What happened next was so disturbing that I almost toppled the cart. Can you guess what happened? She laughingly said that it was alright and that was just how he was. I was through. He laughed and threw the whole thing in his mouth. Can you see why I was not laughing though? I left that job not too long after that.

My sisters, why, why, why would you go to that level of living? Understand that your way of living is produced primarily by your way of thinking; as you think, so you become in your heart. Your heart then pushes out into your life what it believes. Your way of thinking is primarily determined by your influences: what you listen to, who you listen to, what you speak, what you look at regularly and so on.

You can set the course of your living by your influences, good or bad. I admonish you to choose the good. Your choices or decisions decide your influences and your passion will drive your decisions. It is like this. Experts tell you that if you want to lose weight, change your lifestyle. Your style of living determines your weight gain or loss. Likewise, if you are not enjoying your life, change your passions.

There are good men out there that will make excellent husbands. Mr. Right is out there. Do not limit yourself or God in what is possible for a good relationship to develop. Trust God that you will have days of heaven on earth with a husband that will cherish you, love you, appreciate you, stay with you, build with you and win with you.

Do not get into the mindset that all the good men are already married and if you need a good man you will have to take him from his wife. First of all, everything that glitters is not gold. He might look good, dress well and say the right things but you do not live with him. Remember Dr. Jekyll and Mr. Hyde?

Secondly, God has not called us to break up marriages. If he put them together then do not tear them apart or else you will pit yourself against God. How can you build something successful for yourself when you destroyed something that God put together? Thirdly, if he is looking outside of his relationship for something to satisfy a part of him, when he becomes unsatisfied with you, what do you think he will do? Come on and love right my sisters, love right. I pray that as you continue to read this Movement that something in you will be empowered and encouraged. Read on.

Depreciation versus Appreciation

Influences will *help* you set your self-worth. This means that you will depreciate or appreciate in value based on who and what influences you. But let us be clear on this at the beginning. You set the value for yourself now, not your parents, friends, exes, teachers, bosses, Music Industry, Hollywood, Madison Avenue or TV shows. They affect you based on how much credence you give to them. But at the end of the day you are the setter, you set the value. If you lower the estimation of yourself and call yourself a female dog then *that* is your estimation of yourself. My question to you is this, what value have you placed on yourself?

Have you ever seen an auctioneer do his thing? He talks a bit about the item then he asks for the bidding to be opened at a certain price. Every day the little auctioneer in your head brings certain items to your mind, talks about them and then asks for you to open the bid at a certain amount. He says do I hear a high value for the negative words your parents said over you. What about the hurt you experienced from your exes? "Do I hear a high value", he asks? It is up to you to open the bidding and set a value on what they did or said.

Whatever value you place on the negative words or actions will depreciate the positive words or actions to a certain degree. If you are bogged down with failed relationships because you placed such a high value on what happened in your past relationships, it will depreciate the value you place on yourself for good relationships going forward. This will affect what you can receive from God and others. For example, if you feel like a failure because you've been divorced 5 times, when God brings Mr. Right into your life you automatically begin to imagine that the relationship will fail. Once you impose that self-depreciating sub conscious mentality upon the relation-ship it will take on water. Ships that take on water usually sink.

That is how important influences are. My suggestion is that you begin to look at who and what is influencing you and determine how much value you place on them. If they are negative or anti-God influences then it is time to reduce their value to zero. If they are going to help you to live a more productive and enjoyable God-purposed life, then raise the value. Turn your life around today and see a new you by tomorrow. Don't live with regret later on, live with discipline today. I like how Jim Rohn talked about discipline and regret when he said that the pain of discipline weighs ounces but that the pain of regret weighs tons (Rohn, 1991). Live with purpose, live with discipline, live with a high value of yourself. And all my sisters said, "Amen!"

Genesis 2 for the Agaphilerosa

In the Book of Genesis 2 God does some things that I believe every woman should take note of very carefully. I thank Dr. Dollar, Dr. Munroe and Apostle T. Allen Stringer for allowing the Holy Spirit to use them to open the doors of revelation on this one.

First of all we see that God planted the garden and then He placed the man in the garden. That garden contained all that the man would need to survive and thrive. In it he would have food, water, gold and precious stones, and a tree of life to sustain him forever. As a matter of fact, he was going to expand the purpose of God all through the earth from generation to generation beginning in the garden.

However, observe with me how you arrived on the scene my sister. (Thank you Apostle Stringer for this door). God created the heavens, the earth, the light, heavenly bodies, plant life, water life, air life, ground life, man life and allowed them all to begin their operation in the earth. But He had an ace in the hole (really in the side). When everything was finished and the garden prepared and the man equipped and anointed, God stepped in again to finish his masterpiece. (*Michelangelo ain't got nothin' on God*, in my College Park voice). What He began in Adam's side He now completed with the precision of the Master Designer that He is. With all of creation watching, except Adam, who was sleeping of course, God formed, fashioned, shaped and designed the masterpiece of masterpieces; the woman.

My sister, you are the crème de la crème of creation, the epitome of all that is beautiful, the gem of the universe, the apple of God's eye, the darling of design, the jackpot and the grand prize. You put the *Wow* in wow, the *Oh My God* in omg, the *Got to be Almighty* in, well you know.

You were on display from the beginning. Can you imagine all the angels, the living creatures who guard the throne, the animals, and the birds, anything that had sight waiting to see what the omega of creation would look like? Then it happened. She was created and Adam awoke and saw that God had reserved His finest for him. A sense of awe and wonder came upon him, then smiles, then laughter then applause all around. I imagine Adam saying, "God, You outdid Yourself this time. Man was a great work, but this woman is by far Your greatest creation."

Sisters, this is your heritage. Is it any wonder that the previous masterpiece (Lucifer) would be jealous of you and would begin to plot your demise? Is it any wonder that even today that old Lucifer would continue his war against you and whatever you have? Did you not read the Book of Revelation 12 where he is still waiting to destroy whatever you can produce? You think it is just coincidence and do not realize that your hater from the Garden of Eden hates you even more today.

He doesn't like you, he hates you and wants to break you. He wants to take away the awesome beauty which you have in God and replace it with his ugliness of a life. He wants you to see yourself through the eyes of the world rather than the eyes of the Word. He wants to make you think less of who you are rather than find out that you are indeed God's finest. He wants to ruin your ability to love right so that you will never receive the love that God has prepared for you.

Look with me for a moment as I compare the garden to your marriage. God plans and plants a marriage in a particular place with a special someone just for you. Within that marriage are all the nutrients (food and water) that you will need as a woman. In that marriage you will have all the necessary financial resources (gold and precious stones) necessary to spread the purpose for which you were born. In that marriage you will be fed eternal or continual life (from the tree of life).

Now you see why it is important to not get hooked up with the wrong Adam. In order to love him and honor him the right way in the garden he must be the right one for you. To try to love the wrong one in a right way is to risk forfeiting the purpose for which your marriage was created. What God has joined together has purpose.

Your marriage is designed to keep you full and protect you from being empty. Everything that Adam and Eve needed to be full was right there in the garden. Look at all the trees.

They were full of fruit, pleasant to the eyes and good for satisfying all hunger pangs.

Sisters, choose the husband that God has for you because he will be the one designed to fill you up with all that you need in every way that you need it. You will not have to eat from another woman's garden if you feed yourself properly from your own. Wise women learn how to cultivate the fruit that is in their own garden and not waste time cultivating someone else's fruit tree. Give your trees what they need and they will feed you well with fruit designed especially for you. Trust me. God designed you and so He knows exactly what you need to satisfy every hunger pang that you could ever have.

One of the things that you as a wife must do is dwell with your husband according to honor. Husbands need honor. Ask yourself questions like, "What type of honor should I give to him, when should it be given and how should it differ or change over time?" You can invariably miss out on many meals from your garden if you are not paying attention to what it needs. You can even go hungry and it will be your own fault for doing so. If a gardener has trees and never attends to them or eats their fruit, who can he blame for going hungry? At that point he takes the blame on himself.

Your marriage is also designed to keep you from being thirsty. A woman cannot live for a long time without water and neither will your marriage survive without the necessary moisture. Notice that the rivers began in the garden and not elsewhere. As a wife you should never leave home thirsty because you may end up at someone else's river trying to satisfy a thirst that should be quenched in your own garden by your own rivers.

As I was going over the text I thought that it would be good to hear from the rivers themselves and see what they could possibly mean for all of us but particularly my sisters.

The first river is called Pison and it carries the meaning of increase. When Eve arrived on the scene she drank from waters of increase. Women should want a husband that can show them how he plans to increase the resources in the relationship. If all he does is decrease you then he may not be the one for you or he may be out of season for a relationship. Put him back on the tree to ripen up a bit. If a man is not bringing you "Pison" he may be bringing you some type of poison. Pison increases life expectancy; poison decreases life expectancy. Do not ever be afraid or ashamed to ask a potential husband how he intends to increase the resources in the family. Drink from Pison, not from poison.

The second river is called Gihon and it carries the meaning of bursting forth. This name or title is also used for a spring where King Solomon was anointed and proclaimed as king. Change will burst forth at Gihon: status, career, family, responsibilities, basically your life will come under heavier construction upon meeting Mr. Right. When you both meet you will discover that you both are anointed for each other and things will begin to burst forth from you both. Adam and Eve were anointed for each other and so should the both of you.

He must also recognize that he is dealing with a queen. A real king will know how to make you feel like a queen. If you marry someone who is not a king, then you are gambling with your moisture needs. This will leave you and your relationship dry, thirsty and dehydrated.

The third river is called Hiddekel and it means rapid. It is the very same river by which Daniel received 3 things: a powerful vision, a delayed answer and great spiritual victory. A woman should require that her husband be a man with vision. Nothing makes a man mess up more than when he gets sidetracked from his vision. A God breathed vision will give him purpose and help him to focus.

Sometimes answers get held up for various reasons. In this case Daniel's answer was delayed for 21 days as the Prince of Persia fought against the angel who had the answer. Daniel's vision came with spiritual opposition and so will your husband's vision. God sent the answer to Daniel rapidly but manifestation took some time. However, Daniel did not quit and he did not give up and neither must you. When you drink from Hiddekel it will empower you to stay the course so that you can receive rapid spiritual victory against your enemies.

The fourth river was called Euphrates and it means fruitfulness. When you drink from the Euphrates you will be fruitful. Every relationship God purposes have an anointing by God to be fruitful to benefit someone else. If there are seed and eggs involved, then it is supposed to be fruitful. Even if there are no human babies there are still many things that you can be fruitful in so that you can be a blessing to others. Sisters make sure that your prospective husband is a fruitful man and wants to see your marriage become fruitful enough to bless others.

Your husband must understand your moisture needs and he must be able to handle them. Sisters, we as men are not sufficient in ourselves to love you right. We need God for that. He can and He will teach us how to love you but then we have to remain focused on what we are taught about you. Remember, God made you last so that you can be first. Notice, God made the garden and the rivers while Adam watched but when he made you everything and everyone was already in place.

You are designed to be a life giver and a life receiver. When God created man, the Love Manual called man a living soul or a communicating soul. Things that are alive communicate. When Eve was on the inside she could not communicate with Adam. That was not on a level he could handle at the time. She had to be brought out to his level so that she could help him. Adam did not even know what he had on the inside of him. Most men don't. You have to help them.

Humans were created to communicate. That is why communication in a marriage is like blood in a body. Everything that God created communicates in its own way but only humans communicate like God, Genesis 1:26-27. We are created in His image and likeness so whatever we are doing we are communicating who we are to others. That is why it is imperative to choose a husband who communicates well, who can communicate life and not just talk.

The final note for this section is a scriptural nuance that you may not have seen before. To me it reveals how great our God is and how important marriage between a man and a woman is to Him. Look at the Book of Revelation 21:9 to 22:5. The angel announces to the apostle John that he should come and see the **bride**, the wife of Jesus the Lamb of God. What John sees is a city containing the finest **gold** and **precious stones**, **food**, **water** and the **tree of life**. In that city God is the light.

Beloved, what God began to do in the Garden of Eden He expands and culminates in the New Jerusalem as we move into eternity. Open your eyes sisters to see what God is doing so that you do not love your husband in the wrong manner. Marriage is important to God and when you love the right way the marriage relationship can get to its final destination; success. Agaphileros is the right way to love.

Leave the e-v-i-l alone and l-i-v-e

The tree of the knowledge of good and evil will also be present in every marriage. Genesis 2:9, and 17. Your obedience to what God says will protect you from disaster and determine your success in the marriage relationship. Other voices will speak and say things that oppose what God has said. Their philosophy will sound good, their reasoning will be interesting, they may even quote a scripture out of context, but do not be deceived. Deception will dismantle God's design for your marriage leaving you as a statistic of failure wondering what happened. Leave the forbidden alone because it will bring death; *cessation* of purpose and *separation* from God's best. God wants you to have the best of the Garden so leave that tree alone.

All knowledge is not good knowledge and you have to choose well what to know and what not to know. There are many situations that are presented to you daily that brings negative knowledge your way. You will be tempted to try what you should not try because others have. You may surmise that you can try it and nothing will happen because it worked for someone else. Do not go with that thought.

Sisters, it is best to leave some knowledge alone. You do not have to know everything, especially if it is of an evil nature. The Apostle Paul gives us some great advice when it comes to the topic of what we should spend time thinking upon. Take note of his Thought Recipe: **"For the rest, brethren, whatever is true, whatever is worthy of reverence and is honorable and seemly, whatever is just, whatever is pure, whatever is lovely and lovable, whatever is kind and winsome and gracious, if there is any virtue and excellence, if there is anything worthy of praise, think on and weigh and take account of these things (fix your minds on them)** (Amplified Bible, 1987).

The tree of the knowledge of good and evil is less about God restricting you and more about God protecting you, but you have to choose to think about what you are thinking about. That's knowledge. What have you been thinking about? You have to know what knowledge you are bringing into your mind because good knowledge blesses you and evil knowledge curses you.

If you use Paul's Thought Recipe it will help you to have the marriage of a lifetime. Every marriage has that tree containing evil and as the wife you need to keep that evil knowledge away from your marriage, your family, your mind and fix your mind on what is good.

Here is the progression. Loving right begins with the Love Manual and your relationship to it. This will lead you to thinking right. Thinking right will then lead you to believing right. Believing right will lead you to living right and living right will get you to your destination. Reject evil thoughts and live the Agaphileros Zoe life of God.

Genesis 24 for the Agaphilerosa

The Book of Genesis 24 is the 4th longest chapter by verse count in the King James Version of the Love Manual. The 1st is Psalms 119, the 2nd is Numbers 7 and the 3rd is Deuteronomy 28. The 1st deals with the Word and the profound respect it deserves in all relationships. The 2nd deals with offerings and giving. The 3rd deals with blessings and curses which stem from obedience and disobedience and the 4th deals with how to choose a spouse and have a God ordained marriage. There are many ways to choose a spouse but if you want to do it the way that the Love Manual advises then I suggest you stick and stay with passages like Genesis 24.

The significance of choosing a spouse and having a God ordained marriage can be seen in what precedes the 4th longest chapter in length. The word of God is first and is necessary for all the things we build and for everything we believe including choosing a spouse and having a God ordained marriage. As a matter of fact, everything that we talk about is birthed in the word of God then manifested in our lives.

Offerings and giving is second and shows how much emphasis God places on being a giver even before you are a spouse. If you are not practicing giving then you certainly are not practicing receiving. Virtuous women are great givers.

The third passage reveals the promises and the warnings that you can reference for your marriage and in addition, shows how to walk in obedience with each other. You are designed to be blessed and not cursed. Walk in the blessings of obedience and you will not fulfill the disobedience that brings the curse.

Genesis 24 is the story of how Abraham sent his chief servant to choose a spouse for his son. I cannot dissect all of it in this Movement but only what pertains to your choices as an agaphilerosa. As a woman and an agaphilerosa, *you* still have to choose someone. Just because a man comes to you and says that God told him you are his wife does not mean that he is your husband. On the other hand, just because he does not meet every single criterion that you have locked away in your mind does not mean that he is not your husband. Let's look at some of the things that you should look for from this chapter and also see how God moved on behalf of that relationship and hopefully yours as well.

Rebekah was an answer to prayer. Have you positioned yourself to be an answer to prayer for a God fearing man or are you just waiting for him to ride up on a white horse all dressed in shining armor? The servant Eliezer was pro-active in his duties to find this chaste woman, God was pro-active to answer his prayer and you should be pro-active in your preparation for his arrival.

You can prepare for your husband by being someone that prays. (Selah: pause and calmly think about that). It is a shame that we still have to encourage people to pray but if Jesus had to do it who are we? Pray sister, pray. Don't be chosen by a wolf in sheep's clothing that *preys* on you, and then become a woman who prays. Pray now so that you do not become a prey.

When Jessy had to pray about me she said one prayer and by morning time had an answer. That is phenomenal when it works like that but sometimes you will have to stay before the Lord with your faith and his word. Before I move on to the next thing let me say this just in case you skimmed over it. **Pray!**

No man had known her. This is a good thing for her because she was saving herself sexually for the husband that God had for her. But even beyond that, no man really **knew** who she was. Have you ever been with someone who just did not click with you, they just seemed not to really know you? They looked the part and that excited you but when you began to converse with them and build a relationship with them, you realize that they really do not know you and are not absorbing the real you.

Sisters, most men will never really know you because they do not have that key to you. That husband that God has for you can access those inner files locked behind a plethora of codes and passwords. He is supposed to know you.

She was willing to go the extra mile. Sisters, Rebekah was not lazy, she was actively engaged in productive behavior. Eliezer prayed to find a woman at work. You can tell a lot about a woman when you see her work ethic. Lazy cannot attract kings, and please do not try to hide lazy behind tired, weight loss, weight gain, lack of education, loss of a job, having a baby out of wedlock, lack of funds, depression, death of a loved one, etc. Lazy people are just plain lazy and lazy people live by excuses. Most likely you will not be found if you are lazy, you will just be seen.

In Proverbs 18:22 it talks about the man that finds a wife not sees a woman. Wives are found but lazy women are only seen. Rebekah not only offered Eliezer water to drink but brought water up the steps of the well to feed 10 animals which had the most voracious of water appetite; camels. It is one thing to feed a man but to feed a camel, now that is something else. That was some kind of a virtuous woman.

She moved with haste to solve an unannounced problem. Are you a problem creator or a problem solver? Sisters, don't just look at problems, always have a mind to be a solver of problems. You can utilize both parts of your brain at the same time. Put one to work on the solution and you will get ahead in life. Once you have found the solution move with haste. Men from God are not looking to marry a problem creator, no, they want to marry a problem solver.

She was designed with everything that he would need to finish his assignment. Powerful! Sisters, make sure you are the kind of wife that has what a good man needs in order for him to grow into a better man and become what he is called to become. This goes back to your anointing and design. It is to make him not break him. When God and a good wife get a hold to a good man, the world will feel the impact.

Eliezer held his peace until she had done the entire task that he had asked the Lord for her to do. Sisters, be patient in well doing because in due season you will reap an Isaac if you do not faint. Be a starter but also be a finisher. Finish what God calls you to do because someone might just be watching you. Also, be patient when choosing a spouse. Turn off the biological clock and be patient. Sometimes a temporary comes dressed in permanent clothing. Wait on the Lord.

Oh, and by the way, those 10 camels had a *mall* on their backs. They were loaded with clothes, jewelry and gifts for the virtuous woman. The other ladies who were saying things like, "She so crazy to be running up and down the steps to feed that man's camels. Not me!" and "She always does too much. It doesn't take all of that", probably were quite upset when she started to reap the benefits of her labor. Don't hang with the haters, hang out with the other virtuous women.

Psalms 16:11

"You will show me the path of life; in Your presence is fullness of joy, at Your right hand there are pleasures forevermore." Psalms 16:11 (Amplified Bible, 1987). Sisters, I wanted to let you know that God knows how to produce joy and pleasures in a marriage. Who do you think invented marriage and sex? God did.

Bear in mind however, that to enjoy them both, you have to bring Him (God) into the marriage relationship. They are in His presence and at His right hand. Over the years, some have attempted to distort what were intended to be a tremendous benefit to everyone (marriage and sex). This distortion is a diabolical deviation from what was intended to bless both the man and the woman. It's time to love right and get the fullness of joy back into our marriages.

Relationship Killers

Some relationship killers are activated before you begin a relationship and others while you are within a relationship. Some are the same for male and female and some are specific to one or the other. Either way they are designed to end or at least maim the relationship so that it will not complete its purpose. Let us look at 3 that are common to both male and female, then another 2 that are common to the woman.

Unforgiveness: It is a big need in relationships, it is vitally important in order to be a healthy person and to have a healthy relationship. It can eat away at your soul, hinder your physical health and unhinge your life from the success designed for it. True forgiveness does not ask you to forget but it does ask you to release people from what they have done to you or others. It does you no good to hold forgiveness from others as this does nothing to help them or yourself.

But, you say, "This is not the first time they did me like this". Well how many times should you forgive someone? Jesus said 490 times if you want to keep a record. That is per incident by the way. Who has time for that? Would you like to sleep better at night? How about keeping your blood pressure down? Why not bypass strokes and aneurisms? Jesus was a forgiver even at the point of being murdered. Who have you not forgiven lately?

Degrading Speech: It's not funny to put down someone by calling them outside of their names in a degrading way. I used to be like that, especially in school where I could make people cry with my words. I represented my initials very well at that time. I have my mouth under much greater control now, blessing and not cursing, and I am ever striving to see the fruit of the Book of James 3:2, **"For we all often stumble and fall and offend in many things. And if anyone does not offend in speech (never says the wrong things) he is a fully developed character and a perfect**

man, able to control his whole body and to curb his entire nature" (Amplified Bible, 1987).

Thank God for those of you that are able to say the right things all the time but for those of us that are still growing into that level, we strive to speak the right words so that we do not kill any more good relationships in our lives. It is hard enough to get a good relationship going, and then to kill it with the wrong words is truly disheartening.

Lying: Women usually pay attention to detail and that makes you sisters pretty good at discerning the lies of men. However, some men will gain knowledge of you to the point that they will also know when you are being untruthful. Yes you do stutter, look away from us and act fidgety when making up a story at times. Some of us do pay attention and take mental notes, but may not say anything for a while.

In addition, some men are unforgiving (wrongly so), when it comes to a woman lying to them, especially if they have been true to the woman. Lying is a work of the devil so it should not be encouraged or tolerated at any time. Jesus was manifested to destroy the works of the devil. So to avoid killing a good relationship, tell the truth, even if it hurts you. Practice "truthing" not lying.

I am sure you have some things that you want to keep a secret but there are some secrets that you need to tell. If it can affect the longevity and life of the relationship or can cause major damage to the ship, you should consider revealing it. Of course, develop the relationship before you begin telling all of your secrets. The reason that it is a secret is because it may bring you more pain if it is revealed, or it may embarrass you, or it just might upset you. Either way, you cannot love without trusting so if he is trust worthy, then trust him.

Punishing: You know how it goes. "Ralph" forgets to do something that you know he should have done or forgets an anniversary and so now you have to punish him for being a forgetful husband. No food, no communication and no sex are on the punishment list. The excuses begin to roll in: headaches, PMS and not feeling well are some of the more common excuses. You are probably smiling while you are reading this because you know someone who has done this before, haven't you? Let me sound an alarm, raise a flag and overall warn you about something. You reap what you sow just not in the same quantity.

As men we may not have PMS and headaches but there are ways that we can get our needs met when we are being punished. Some men simply satisfy themselves through pornography and self-gratification. Other men call up a former flame or some new friend that can pacify them. Some men will deliberately go hang out with the boys and head out to the club knowing full well what will happen at the "club". By the way, what happens at the club does not always stay at the club either. He may bring something home that he does not even know he "picked up".

Punishment works differently between kids and husbands. You could very well drive the man away into the waiting arms of his demise through punishing him. My advice to you is to simply weigh the situation and see how to make it better. That is why you have the Love Manual, the Holy Spirit and communion. So, giving "Ralph" the silent treatment will not help him. You will just be establishing negative parameters within the relationship. Does God give you the silent treatment when you mess up?

Emasculating and not Educating:

This one was given to me by the Holy Spirit while writing the first book, "Agaphileros A". I saved it for last on purpose. There are too many emasculators and not enough educators in relationships today. First of all, let me tell you what emasculation means. It carries the meaning of castrating, depriving of strength or vigor, to weaken and to make effeminate, especially psychologically.

Relative to a man that is being emasculated, you are

making him weak, effeminate and cutting off his manhood (castrating him). There are certain things that you can say to a man and do to a man that will emasculate him psychologically. Saying things that compare him negatively to other men, his dad and other men who he cannot measure up to is emasculation. Making mention of his sexual ability in a degrading manner is emasculation. Speaking down concerning his efforts as a father, Christian, employee, business man, entrepreneur, minister, visionary, and anything else like that is emasculation.

Listen sisters, we already know that we are not perfect and depending on who is talking we are already being castrated by certain sectors of society and social media. The last thing we want is to be emasculated by our wives or women. If there is any place that we should be built up and encouraged is when we are with you. You are our last resort. If you break us down then what are we? Not much. We become weak and lose strength. A man without his manhood is not a full man.

My suggestion is that you chose education. Impart knowledge, and the men that are teachable will grow and become better. Every situation is a teachable moment. Why do you think that I stress the importance of being teachable so much? And why would you marry a man that is not teachable in the first place?

Jessy taught me more about how to be the man she needed than any man ever taught me about how to be a man. Are you teaching him or shouting at him? Are you building him up or talking down to him? Teach. The dating period is a good place to determine if your man is teachable. Does he take to your various teaching methods and most importantly, does he become better from them? If he is teachable he is keepable. So refrain from being an emasculator and become an educator. You will be a much happier woman and will believe that you have the best husband in the world. That is a good thing. He will think the world of you just like I thought of my

Jessy.

Qualities to look for in a husband

*He will **love** you like Christ loves the Church.* Ephesians 5:25. This piece of advice is worth the cost of this project that you are now reading. If nothing else, be absolutely sure that your "husband to be" knows and understands how Christ loves the Church. I can write a volume just on this verse but to condense it here I will say this.

The first word is "**husbands**". He must be husband material. When Eve showed up, Adam had everything in place by the grace of God to meet her needs. I did not say that he was rich although he was. You do not *need* a rich man although it would be nice. What you *need* is a man who is equipped to meet your needs.

Not the superfluous needs purported by the world, but the needs that God knows that you as a woman presently have and will have in the future. Note carefully how he attends to your needs when you are getting to know each other. If it is all about his needs then you need to move on.

The next key word is "**love**" agape, not eros. He will love you without conditions. He will not bring a lot of garbage talk to the table about what you have to do or become for him. Jesus became what we needed because He loved us first. Your agaphileroso should be loving you first and seeking to be there for you in whatever way that he can.

Real love is something that grows and never plateaus therefore he will also be a student of love. You don't want a dropout from the school of love, you want a currently enrolled student who will learn it, master it then improve on it just for you.

The next key word is "**wives**". He has to understand that when he finds a wife he must forsake **all** others. Just recently there was a story here in the greater Atlanta area about a man who was married but had a mistress who he had living in another house that he bought and she was also driving a vehicle that was in his name. She found out about a vacation that the man and his wife were about to take and bought some handcuffs, obtained a gun, went to the home of the married couple, kidnapped the wife, shot her to death then shot herself.

Marriage is supposed to be a 'closed' relationship. It is leaving all others and cleaving to each other. He has to believe in keeping it closed to other women so that there is no opportunity to destroy what you have built together. When you open a 'closed' relationship you invite in the curse. Once the curse is in, the end is near. Our first mother Eve did just that, and when Adam signed off on the opening, the curse became active. Thank God for Jesus.

The next key word is "**gave**" which is a characteristic of love. Remember when you were a little girl and a little boy said he liked you? The next thing that he did was give something to you, didn't he? That is what love does, it seeks to give. Lust seeks to take so be on the lookout for that. And on top of that, Jesus gave all of Himself. Why? That is what we required in order to be reconnected to God. Does the man in your life understand that he has to be willing to give all that he has in order to love you right? Because if he is to love you right then he must be willing to give you it all. To take all from you is the wrong way to love and he disqualifies himself.

*He will **wash** you with God's word and not **dirty** you with his words.* Ephesians 5:26. Here comes a bonus. What a man says to you, about you and on your behalf must make you feel as if he is washing you with love. Do you know that warm, loving feeling you get when he speaks certain types of words? How you can feel your entire insides just melting away? This should be a growing feeling and not a diminishing, fleeting feeling. (Yeah, I like to set the bar high. You will thank me later).

Remember, marriage before God is a permanent covenant relationship designed to last until the final breath and it should grow into something that can bless the world in some way. Maybe you have dealt with men in the past who did not know how to speak to you with love on a regular ongoing basis and they caused you to start and stop, again and again, like a vehicle with the wrong gasoline. Since his words are like gasoline to your vehicle, you should be full of premium all the time. Your spirit, psychological being and physical body should read "F" whenever he is with you. So teach him how to fill your tank if he does not know how.

The power of life and death is in the tongue according to the Love Manual recorded in Proverbs 18:21. I once heard someone say that you turn on the life cycle or the death cycle based on the words that you choose to say. The husband that you should be looking for is one who is constantly turning on the life cycle. The reason why this is important is because there are only 2 cycles to turn on. His mouth is like a washing machine that has 2 cycles (and yours is as well). Every time he communicates he should be turning on the life cycle. As a matter of fact, he should be washing you in the life cycle before you even venture into marriage. If he does not know how, well, you know what to do.

He will desire you to be **holy** *and* **without blemish** *before the Lord.* Ephesians 5:27. A man that really wants you for life will want you to be holy before God. Holiness is simply the art of being set apart for God; being devoted for the service of God. He will desire it for both of you because without it, you will not be able to *see* God, particularly in your relationship. The Book of Hebrews 12:14 says, "**Pursue peace with all people, and holiness, without which no one will see the Lord.**" Holiness is your access key to seeing God work in your relationship and that is what you want.

A good husband also knows that if his future wife is devoted to the Lord, he is going to get a woman set apart for him and the Lord Jesus. However, you should not use holiness as a cloak of deception to get your own way and you should not use the church to keep you from your husband.

That is not agaphileros. Choose the right husband in the beginning and you will not have to resort to the wrong type of behavior along the way.

To be without blemish is to be faultless. Just as Jesus dealt with all of our faults, your husband will properly handle any faults that you possess. He will not be the one to blame you for every little thing but he will be ready to help you to fix any problem that may have been your fault.

What is a fault? A fault can be a flaw in any area of your life and most everyone you meet has them. You do not want to be reminded of every little flaw you possess, especially by someone you plan to spend the rest of your life with. In Isaiah 58:12 we are told that the Lord raises up his people as repairers of breaches and restorers of paths. Make sure your intended husband is a repairer and a restorer and not a fault finder.

He will love you like his own body by **nourishing** and **cherishing** you. Ephesians 5:28-29. If he nourishes and cherishes you it will be evident by the way he treats you. Suffice it to say that if there is any indication of violence towards you there is a major lack of nourishing and cherishing on his part. A good man is not going to abuse the woman in his life through words and hurtful actions. Never become so desperate for love that you ignore the traits of abuse and walk into what could be the final relationship of your life here on earth. Use your God given intuition and wisdom to get out of any situation that may cost you more than you are willing to pay.

He will **appoint** and **agree** with you for the purpose of the relationship. Amos 3:3. "**Do two walk together except they make an appointment and have agreed?**" (Amplified Bible, 1987) To build together there must be some discussions about appointments where agreements are hashed out concerning what it is to be built and the roles that are to be played. Not just time appointments but role appointments, who does what. This way, you can walk together having agreed upon responsibilities.

Building a marriage? Discuss, appoint and agree about what it is going to become. Building a family? Discuss, appoint and agree about raising the kids. Building a business? Discuss, appoint and agree about the parameters of the undertaking. Building Agaphileros? Discuss, appoint and agree about what to work on, sacrifice and change. To refuse to discuss, appoint and agree may bring cussing, disagreement and disappointment. Also, be willing to make adjustments to the appointments along the way so that you can continue to walk in agreement.

He will never bring **shame** to you in public or private. Matthew 1:18-19. He will be a just man like Joseph, Mary's husband. One thing that he will not do is increase drama. He will be a peace maker. I just love the way Joseph was considering Mary's status in the public eye. He was caring and considerate of her feelings and of how she might be seen by others. (Oh God, raise up more men like this and less men that do the opposite). It is a sign of relationship maturity on Joseph's behalf that he did not want to do what he had to do in public. Thanks to Facebook, Twitter, Instagram and the rest of them, you can tell the whole world about a person and humiliate them in a moment. Talk about a public example? How about an international example?

If he is a person that constantly spends time talking about people in a public forum, then he is not ready for you at this time. Put him back where you found him. Remember, if he is dogging out the past girlfriends or wives on his social media pages or to you, he will do the same to you later on. In addition, if he does something in a public place or on a public website that you feel shamed about, mention it to him. His response will let you know if you should move forward or head back to the proverbial drawing board. If he does this repeatedly then allow me to repeat myself; put him back where you found him.

He should have, or at least, should want to have a

sensitive ear to the Holy Spirit. Matthew 1:20. You will appreciate a husband with the ability to hear from God. During my marriage to Jessy and even before we were married, there were those times that I knew I had heard from the Lord, e.g. concerning the move from Trinidad to Connecticut and then to Atlanta, the 1st home we bought, allowing her to teach me about how to love her, giving her the advantage, et al. Sisters, we may not always hear it right because we are still working on our hearing, but if we are hearing that is a plus. A man who hears the Lord, who can find? You.

He will be **preserved** by God just for you and not hidden away from you. Proverbs 18:22. God is in the preservation business. You have to believe that He is because some of you are going to require a special man that only God can deliver to you. You know what I mean. The verse said that **he** will be looking to find you.

In Genesis, God brought Adam to Eve but in Proverbs, the man was looking for his wife. Let him do some looking while you make your virtue visible. Some of you may say that there are fewer and fewer good men out there so why wait. Some may even say, "Bump preservation, my clock is ticking. It's every woman for her own self." Make that move, right now baby, as Shalamar counseled.

Let me tell you the problem with that. If you are choosing then God is chilling. When you learn how to chill in God, He will choose for you and with you. If you choose and it backfires, guess who has to pick up the pieces? To choose a good man on your own is like playing the lottery; if you win that is great but 99.9% of the people who play lose. Your odds are not good. To allow God to choose for you and with you is a win-win. This helps to take the pressure off your shoulders so that you can focus on being a virtuous woman.

Also, there is a man in the Love Manual called Elijah who had a bad day and complained that he was the only one left who wanted to serve God. One of the things that God told him was that He had 7,000 knees that had not bowed down to the enemy. Now I say to you my lovely sisters, God has many men that He has not brought out of production as yet and one of them belongs to you.

He may bring him in a way that you are not accustomed to. He may look very different than what you always thought that you would see in a husband. He may be of another culture or color or age or financial level, but if you limit God, you may disqualify yourself right out of what He has preserved for you. Loving a husband the right way is too important for you to do the wrong thing to get one. Now chill.

Grace Nuggets

As I wrap up this important Movement I would like to leave some parting words with you. A real woman is graced for her man. If he is not teachable and does not bear an equal yoke with you before marriage, then you should probably move on until he is or until the right one shows up. God has many good men in His kingdom so trust God.

In true love, agreement does not come before advantage. Jesus demonstrated His love for us by giving us the advantage first. We then agree with Him for what He has done and then seek to do the same for Him. Become a woman that loves to give the advantage and you will attract a man that loves to do the same. Giving the advantage is the pinnacle of selflessness and the antithesis or the direct opposite of selfishness.

There is a dilemma that most women face and it is this; should I choose a husband with my physical eyes or with my spiritual eyes? Let me help you. Being selfless is always better than being selfish or self-more. Always choose every day to serve God and others through selflessness. Why? Because your self-effort will cause you to choose what you think is best for you which is the person who can give the most to you. But the grace of God will cause you to possess what is best for you, which is the person who can receive the most from you. It is in this position that you will begin to receive more than you could have ever imagined from the person that you freely gave all that you could. God will not give you someone to hurt you, He will give you someone to help you.

The world has a discordant sound (one that is disagreeable to the Love Manual) when it comes to choosing a spouse. Choose not to listen to them. The Lord has already gone ahead of you and has chosen your Isaac. The Holy Spirit has anointed him to be everything that you need. Remove the limits you may have placed upon God the Father and see how He can give you someone that you do not even think you deserve.

What are the limits you ask? Where is he, when will you meet, what is his race, his age, his education, his social status, etc. Take the limits off and live the limitless life.

I have heard that a woman's basic needs vary by many factors and psychologists have determined that these are essential: Security, Affection, Communication, Spiritual Leadership, Affirmation, Honesty, Family commitment and Purpose. She also wants to laugh, feel comfortable and be sincerely complimented. She does not want to be criticized, abused, left alone all the time, feel unwanted, be cheated on, be lied to, be betrayed and such like. Amazingly enough sisters, when you love right, these are all taken care of through seedtime and harvest. This is why I wrote this book because if we can fix life at the love level, we can have better and lifetime marriages. Love right ladies, love right.

Take Aways M5

- ✓ Never be so desperate that you invite Mr. Wrong into a place that belongs to Mr. Right. Never be so pressured that you give your permanent things to some temporary person.

- ✓ The Greek version of the word "husband" from the Love Manual said that a husband is how you distinguish an adult man from a boy. Never ask a boy to do a husband's job.

- ✓ If you are not enjoying your life, change your passions.

- ✓ Influences will *help* you set your self-worth but let us be clear on this at the beginning, you set the value for yourself now.

- ✓ Once you impose that self-depreciating sub conscious mentality upon the relation-ship it will take on water. Ships that take on water eventually sink.

- ✓ Sisters, you are the crème de la crème of creation, the epitome of all that is beautiful, the gem of the universe, the apple of God's eye, the darling of design, the jackpot and the grand prize.

- ✓ To try to love the wrong one in a right way is to risk forfeiting the purpose for which your marriage was created. What God has joined together has purpose.

- ✓ You will not have to eat from another woman's garden if you feed yourself properly from your own. Wise women learn how to cultivate the fruit that is in their own garden and not waste time cultivating someone else's fruit tree.

- ✓ As a wife you should never leave home thirsty because you may end up at someone else's river trying to satisfy a thirst that should be quenched in your own garden by your own rivers.

- ✓ The first river is called Pison and it carries the meaning of increase. Do not ever be afraid or ashamed to ask a potential husband how he intends to increase the resources in the family.

- ✓ The second river is called Gihon and it carries the meaning of bursting forth. When you both meet you will discover that you both are anointed for each other and things will begin to be birth.

- ✓ A real king will know how to make you feel like a queen.

- ✓ The third river is called Hiddekel and it means rapid. It is the very same river by which Daniel received 3 things: a powerful vision, a delayed answer and great spiritual victory.

- ✓ Nothing makes a man mess up more than when he gets side-tracked from his vision.

- ✓ The fourth river was called Euphrates and it means fruitfulness. When you drink from the Euphrates you will be fruitful. Every relationship God purposes have an anointing by God to be fruitful for someone else.

- ✓ Sisters, we as men are not sufficient in ourselves to love you right. We need God for that. Remember, God made you last so that you can be first.

- ✓ Adam did not even know what he had on the inside of him. Most men don't. You have to help them.

- ✓ Deception will dismantle God's design for your marriage leaving you as a statistic of failure wondering what happened.

- ✓ All knowledge is not good knowledge and you have to choose well what to know and what not to know because good knowledge blesses you and evil knowledge curses you.

- ✓ Lazy people are just plain lazy and lazy people live by excuses.

- ✓ In Proverbs 18:22 it talks about the man that finds a wife not sees a woman. Wives are found but lazy women are only seen.

- ✓ When God and a good wife get a hold to a good man, the world will feel the impact.

- ✓ Sometimes a Temporary comes dressed in Permanent clothing. Wait on the Lord.

- ✓ Unforgiveness can eat away at your soul, hinder your physical health and unhinge your heart from the success designed for it.

- ✓ Practice truthing not lying.

- ✓ Emasculation carries the meaning of castrating, depriving of strength or vigour, to weaken, to make effeminate. Relative to a man that is being emasculated, you are making him weak, effeminate and cutting off his manhood (castrating him).

- ✓ You don't want a dropout from the school of love, you want a currently enrolled student who will learn it, master it then improve on it just for you.

- ✓ Marriage is supposed to be a 'closed' relationship. It is leaving all others and cleaving to one. When you open a 'closed' relationship nothing good will happen.

- ✓ If he is to love you right then he must be willing to give you it all. To take all from you is the wrong way to love and he disqualifies himself.

- ✓ Your spirit, psychological being and physical body should read "F" (full) whenever he is with you.

- ✓ The husband that you should be looking for is one who is constantly turning on the life cycle because there are only 2 cycles to turn on. His mouth is like a washing machine that has 2 cycles (and yours is as well).

- ✓ Never become so desperate for love that you ignore the traits of abuse and walk into what could be the final relationship of your life here on earth.

- ✓ To build together there must be some discussions about appointments where agreements are hashed out concerning what it is to be built and the roles to be played. To not discuss may bring cussing, disappointments and disagreements.

- ✓ If he is a person that constantly spends time talking about people in a public forum, then he is not ready for you yet. Put him back where you found him.

- ✓ If you are choosing then God is chilling. When you learn how to chill in God, He will choose for you and with you.

- ✓ Become a woman that loves to give the advantage and you will attract a man that loves to do the same. Giving the advantage is the pinnacle of selflessness and the antithesis of selfishness.

- ✓ Take the limits off and live the limitless life.

- ✓ You may not have to get a divorce from your husband, you may just need to divorce yourself from selfishness and take the limits off of the God you serve. Loving is right and you do not want to be wrong about it.

MOVEMENT 6

A word to the Agaphileroso

God knows how to bless you with the wife you need and place everything you want deep inside her. Learn how to 'mine' her and not just to 'mind' her so that you can go to bed every night with the woman of your dreams.

Teachable, Reachable, Reliable and Keepable

Brothers, this Movement is for you. When a man is teachable he is ready for the highest level of relationships; husband. A husband functions within 2 parts of speech, as a noun and as a verb. When you see one you must see the other. One of the distinguishing features of a husband is that he is a manager (noun) therefore he manages (verb). This is a dictionary definition and I can see its relevance even today. As a husband you should have already been trained to manage your life, your home, your career, your business, your circle and everything at your disposal. The Greek version of the word from the Love Manual said that a husband is how you distinguish an adult man from a boy. Ouch!

I still believe that if God did not call you to be a eunuch or that if you are not serving in a eunuch's role in the world's system, you were born to be a husband. The New Testament verifies this for us with the Greek word "aner". Brothers, "boy" tendencies have to die off so that husband behaviors can show up. Your wife has been waiting for the husband in you to sweep her off her feet. So here is my advice. Put down the video games, discover your purpose, find ways to increase your income, become a student of agaphileros and give the little black book (book for old schoolers and phones for the new school) to your wife. In other words, commit to building a strong marriage and a healthy family as God has instructed in the Love Manual. Anything that you do that does the opposite of this can possibly be considered "boyish" behavior.

Let me also add a personal definition that I believe is accurate. A husband is a leader (noun) and therefore he leads (verb). While a manager handles the operation of a thing, the leader cuts the path for its progress. The success for the operation of marriage today is in the hands of the manager but the vision that produced it and sees its future purpose is in the heart of the leader. Yup.

I heard Dr. Munroe talk about Genesis 2:5 where God could not send rain to grow the plants and the herbs because there was no man or manager in position to handle it at that time. When He created the man or the husbandman, then He could send the harvest. Likewise my brothers, God may be withholding an abundant harvest until you get into position where you can handle it. Look at it as if it was measured in your ability to handle money. If you cannot handle a dollar what makes you think you are ready for 1 million dollars? You may say that you are ready but are you really?

Some men go overboard at their bachelor's party. They say that it is the last time to *get it on* before the ball and chain arrives. They say that they will hang up the player shoes after the party. But getting a wife does not mean that it is time for you to hang up the player shoes. No. Hanging up the shoes takes place beforehand and that shows God that you are ready to handle a wife. Boys play around with temporaries but husbands build around a permanent.

Brothers, here is the reason why you must be teachable. If nobody can tell you anything then eventually you will have nobody to tell anything to. You cannot make the transition from boy to husband without being teachable. Become a student of marriage.

If you are willing to be taught then you can be reached. When God came looking for Adam He could not find him because Adam decided that they should hide since they were naked and exposed. God was not afraid of their nakedness nor was He mad at them. God was only interested in fellowshipping with them. God is looking for leaders that He can give vision to, people that will write the vision and run with it. But God cannot fellowship with you as a leader if He cannot reach you as a student. So to be teachable is to be reachable. Do not hide anymore.

If you are always teachable and always reachable then God and your wife can rely on you being in position no matter what. Your wife can say with confidence, "He is at the gym" or "he is at work." You become reliable: dependable, trustworthy and honest. Never lose those qualities, they are what great husbands and marriages are made of.

If you are teachable, reachable and reliable know that your wife has already determined that you are a keeper. She has hit the jackpot with you. She is not going anywhere and neither will you. A good wife will only seek to enhance what God placed in you. You manage with passion, you lead with vision and you operate with compassion because you are teachable, reachable and reliable. Put all of this together and we have a husband that is keepable. You have earned the title and you will only become better at being who God called you to be. You are keepable my brother and never let anyone tell you any different.

Cut it off

When a child is born the umbilical cord has to be cut. He has never been outside of the womb before so it is a brand new relationship for him. That which nourished him in the old relationship cannot nourish him in the new relationship. Understand that in the womb he was sustained by that umbilical cord but upon exiting he enters a new environment wherein the old cord cannot sustain him anymore and very well might become a hazard.

When a man is married he is technically born again into a relationship that he has never been in before and so must look to cut the old umbilical cords that cannot sustain him in his new environment. Why? It is because God has designed a new umbilical cord to nourish and sustain him.

Just like God chose your mom for you, allow him to choose your wife for you. They both connect with you and nourish you through the natural and proverbial umbilical cord. The connection you make with your wife is a brand new umbilical cord like Adam explained in the Book of Genesis 2:24. As the child is one flesh with the mother while in the womb, so too the husband becomes one flesh with the wife at the marriage covenant. My good friend Joanne Bell says that when a couple has too many cords still connected after marriage, dis*cord* will show up. Discord is a lack of concord or harmony between persons in marriage. Is that the truth or is that the truth?

How many marriages suffer discord because *this* relationship or *that* relationship has not been moved into the proper position for the new relationship? As men we often keep some cords connected to us way too long after meeting the virtuous woman that God designed for us. These can often lead to discord.

Whatever is connected to you will be connected to the marriage relationship. I do not even have to give you a story from the Love Manual about this because we all know someone who brought an old umbilical cord into a new marriage relationship and the marriage relationship did not survive. On some rare occasions, some marriages survive these illegal umbilical connections and prosper anyway (through much work, sacrifice and change), but usually the marriage becomes inharmonious. Brothers, strive to resist the temptation to maintain an illegal umbilical connection after connecting with your wife. That umbilical cord is not worth it. Cut it off!

Genesis 2 for the Agaphileroso

In the Book of Genesis 2 God does some things that I believe every man should take note of very carefully. I thank Dr. Dollar and Dr. Munroe for allowing the Holy Spirit to use them to open the doors of revelation on this one. First of all we see that God planted the garden and then He placed the man in the garden. That garden contained all that the man would need to survive and thrive. In it he would have food, water, gold and precious stones, and a tree of life to sustain him forever. As a matter of fact, he was going to expand the purpose of God all through the earth from generation to generation from the garden, that is, from ground zero.

Look with me for a moment as I compare the garden to your marriage. God plans and plants a marriage in a particular place with a special someone just for you. Within that marriage are all the nutrients (food and water) that you will need as a man. In that marriage you will have all the necessary financial resources (gold and precious stones) necessary to spread the purpose for which you were born. In that marriage you will be fed eternal or continual life (from the tree of life).

God planted your marriage and you were placed into it by God. Now you see why it is important to not bring the wrong *Eve* into your garden. In order to love her the right way in the garden she must be the right one for you. To try to love the wrong one in a right way is to risk forfeiting the purpose for which your marriage was created. What God has joined together has purpose.

The Food, the Water, the Money and the Life.

Your marriage is designed to keep you full and to protect you from being empty. Everything that Adam needed to be full was right there in the garden. Look at all the trees. They were full of fruit, pleasant to the eyes and good for satisfying all hunger pangs.

Brothers, choose the wife that God has for you because she will be the one designed to fill you up with all that you need in every way that you need it. You will not have to eat from another man's garden if you feed yourself properly from your own. Wise men learn how to cultivate the fruit that is in their own garden and not waste time cultivating someone else's fruit tree. Give your trees what they need and they will feed you well with fruit designed especially for you. Trust me. God designed you so He knows exactly what you need to satisfy every hunger need that you could ever have.

One of the reasons that you as a husband must dwell with your wife according to knowledge is so that you can learn her like a gardener learns his fruit trees. Ask yourself questions like, "What type of cultivation does this particular tree require?" "What is the best environment for its growth?" "What pests and dangers should I protect it from?" You can invariably miss out on many meals from your garden if you are not paying attention to what it needs. You can even go hungry and it will be your own fault for doing so. If a gardener has trees and never attends to them or eats their fruit, who can he blame for going hungry? No one but himself.

Your marriage is also designed to keep you from being thirsty. A man cannot live for a long time without water and neither will your marriage survive without the necessary moisture. Notice that the rivers began in the garden and not elsewhere. As a husband you should never leave home thirsty because you may end up at someone else's river trying to satisfy a thirst that should be quenched in your own garden by your own rivers.

Adam had 4 rivers in his garden. A man's basic needs are also 4 per Dr. Dollar: Acceptance, Identity, Security and Purpose. I consider these the moisture needs of a man. Without them you will dry up. Your wife will understand your 4 moisture needs and she will be compatible to them. Remember, God said that it is not good that the man should be alone. If this is the case, and it is, then the water that you need will be in your marriage.

I believe that a man should look for a woman that knows how to make him feel accepted; knows how to help him discover or continue to discover his true identity; knows how to assure him that the home is secured because no *intruders* are welcomed or entertained; and knows how to help him live in his God given purpose. A woman of that caliber is marriage ready and qualifies for *anything* that she desires from you.

When you have identified her as the permanent one, one of the things that you have to do as a husband is to go to the river. The 4 rivers in the Garden of Eden did not flow to Adam. If he was thirsty he had to go to the river. So do not expect that your moisture needs will be met if you just sit back playing video games, posting on social media and eating pizza all day long. A woman of this caliber needs a husband that knows what his basic needs are and is able to drink the water that she will provide for these needs. Go get it brother.

Today we live in a world governed by financial resources. Gold has been a standard of monetary exchange and stability for the longest of times and this is what Adam had access to. It was in his garden and it is in your marriage also. Brothers, you want a wife that understands the value of a dollar and how to apportion it into the places it needs to go.

Not only that, but you want a wife that can see your wealth in you and knows how to help you get it out into the earth. A marriage is not about being broke together; it's about being rich together. Brothers, God has wealth for you and it is inside of your marriage. Remember, he that finds a wife obtains favor from the Lord. She brings the double anointing for increase upon her arrival like a dowry. When she shows up, more favor shows up at the same time.

That is why a temporary is so dangerous because they can steal the wealth that you have in you for your marriage and bring you nothing in return. Your wealth belongs to your permanent. If you marry a temporary you can literally be in covenant with someone who will waste your goods and never help you to bring them to market.

The gold is not for bracelets and earrings for her to show others that she now has some gold. It is for growing enterprise. And brothers, don't waste the gold on your teeth or on chains that are heavy enough to pull you down. It is for investments, in the market place and in the kingdom of God so that you can be amply supplied and have enough to bless others. This is the right way to manage resources; you and your permanent handling what is in your marriage for God's glory. Don't let a temporary use you to blow resources, rather use resources to bless your permanent.

Your marriage contains the tree of life in the midst of it and an EVE to share it with you. This should excite you and make you smile. If nothing else brothers, what you need to be alive and to live long and prosper is planted within the marriage that God placed you in. EVEry marriage that God designed is Zoe (life, in abundance, to the full, till it overflows) in motion and EVE is waiting to share it all with you, EVEry pleasurable experience, EVEry abundant moment, EVEry fullness of purpose and EVEry overflowing joy. They will be actively in pursuit of you in your marriage. (May God give us all marriages like this! So be it).

You are designed to be a life giver and a life receiver. When God created man, the Love Manual called man a living soul or a communicating soul. Things that are alive communicate. The difference between the Adam without the breath of God and the Adam with the breath of God in him is communication. We were created to communicate; we are communicating souls just like God our Father.

That is why communication in a marriage is like blood in a body. Everything that God created communicates in its own way but only humans communicate like God, Genesis 1:26-27. We are created in His image and likeness so whatever we are doing we are communicating who we are to others. That is why it is imperative to choose a wife who communicates well, who can communicate life and not just talk.

Brothers, civilizations are built around natural resources (food, water, earthly substances, things that support life, etc.) and so are good marriages. You will be most happy when you build around these things and build with Eve. God designed it so and He designed her like that just for you. A good wife is someone who understands these things and if she does, then she will never leave you hungry, thirsty, poor or dead.

The final note for this section is a scriptural nuance that you may not have seen before. To me it reveals how great our God is and how important marriage between a man and a woman is to Him. Look at the Book of Revelation from 21:9 to 22:5. The angel announces to the apostle John that he should come and see the **bride**, the wife of Jesus the Lamb of God. What John sees is a city containing the finest **gold** and **precious stones**, **food**, **water** and the **tree of life**.

In that city God is the light. Beloved, what God began to do in the Garden of Eden He expands and culminates in the New Jerusalem as we move into eternity. May God open our eyes to see what He is doing so that we do not continue to love the wrong way. Marriage is important to God and when you love the right way the marriage relationship can get to its final destination; eternity. Agaphileros is the right way to love.

Leave the e-v-i-l alone and l-i-v-e

The tree of the knowledge of good and evil will also be present in every marriage. Genesis 2:9, and 17. Your obedience to what God says will protect you from disaster and determine your success in the marriage relationship. Other voices will speak and say things that oppose what God has said. Their philosophy will sound good, their reasoning will be interesting, they may even quote a scripture out of context, but do not be deceived. Deception will dismantle God's design for your marriage leaving you as a statistic of failure wondering what happened. Leave the forbidden alone because it will bring death; *cessation* of purpose and *separation* from God's best. God wants you to have the best of the Garden so leave that tree alone.

All knowledge is not good knowledge and you have to choose well what to know and what not to know. For example, you hear from an associate that he has a little ménage a trois going on at his home and he believes every man should try it at least once in his life. He has now brought evil knowledge into your space. What do you do?

The tree is waiting there and he has said that the fruit from the tree is delightful and delicious. He is trying to convince you that you are missing out on something fantastic. Choose well my brother. You can choose to reject it and let him know that God is not pleased with that and therefore neither are you, or ask some more questions and stir up that evil desire in you. If you continue to gain knowledge on evil it just might stir a desire which will be fed by more knowledge until you tell yourself that since he tried it and nothing happened, maybe you can try it and see what happens. After all, you are consenting adults.

Now you begin to plan the process of how and when to tell your wife of your evil desire, and the rest is part of your history or the end of your history together. Brothers, it is best to leave some knowledge alone. You do not have to know everything, especially if it is of an evil nature. The Apostle Paul gives us some great advice when it comes to the topic of what we should spend time thinking upon. Take note of his Thought Recipe: **"For the rest, brethren, whatever is true, whatever is worthy of reverence and is honorable and seemly, whatever is just, whatever is pure, whatever is lovely and lovable, whatever is kind and winsome and gracious, if there is any virtue and excellence, if there is anything worthy of praise, think on and weigh and take account of these things (fix your minds on them)** (Amplified Bible, 1987).

The tree of the knowledge of good and evil is less about God restricting you and more about God protecting you, but you have to choose to think about what you are thinking about. That's knowledge. You have to know what knowledge you are bringing into your mind because good knowledge blesses you and evil knowledge curses you. If you use Paul's Thought Recipe it will help you to have the marriage of a lifetime. What have you been thinking about?

Every marriage has that tree containing evil and as the husband you need to keep that evil knowledge away from your marriage, your family, your mind and fix your mind on what is good. Here is the progression. Loving right begins with the Love Manual and your relationship to it. This will lead you to thinking right. Thinking right will then lead you to believing right. Believing right will lead you to living right and living right will get you to your destination. Reject evil thoughts and live the Agaphileros Zoe life of God.

Genesis 24 for the Agaphileroso

The Book of Genesis 24 is the 4th longest chapter by verse count in the King James Version of the Love Manual. The 1st is Psalms 119, the 2nd is Numbers 7 and the 3rd is Deuteronomy 28. The 1st deals with the Word and the profound respect it deserves in all relationships. The 2nd deals with offerings and giving. The 3rd deals with blessings and curses which stem from obedience and disobedience and the 4th deals with how to choose a spouse and have a God ordained marriage. There are many ways to choose a spouse but if you want to do it the way that the Love Manual advises then I suggest you stick and stay with passages like Genesis 24.

The significance of choosing a spouse and having a God ordained marriage can be seen in what precedes the 4th longest chapter in length. The word of God is first and is necessary for all the things we build and for everything we believe including choosing a spouse and having a God ordained marriage. As a matter of fact, everything that we talk about is birthed in the word of God then manifested in our lives.

Offerings and giving is second and shows how much emphasis God places on being a giver even before you are a spouse. If you are not practicing giving then you certainly are not practicing receiving. Good husbands are great givers.

The third passage reveals the promises and the warnings that you can reference for your marriage. In addition, it talks about how to walk in obedience with each other. You are designed to be blessed and not curse. Walk in the blessings of obedience and you will not fulfill the disobedience that brings the curse.

Genesis 24 is the story of how Abraham sent his chief servant to choose a spouse for his son. I cannot dissect all of it in this Movement but only what pertains to your choices as an agaphileroso. Let's look at some of the things that we can learn from Genesis 24 and also see how God moved on behalf of that relationship and hopefully yours as well.

Rebekah was an answer to prayer. Have you been praying about your wife to be or are you just waiting for her to fall from the sky onto your doorstep? The servant Eliezer was pro-active in his duties to find this woman and God was pro-active to answer his prayer.

No man had known her. This is a good thing for her because she was saving herself sexually for the husband that God had for her. But even beyond that, no man had really known who she was. Have you ever been with someone who just did not click with you, they just seemed not to really know you? They looked the part and that excited you but when you began to converse with them and build a relationship with them, you realize that they really do not know you and are not absorbing the real you. Brothers, most women are not really known because they have not met that man of God that can access those inner files locked behind a plethora of codes and passwords. Know thy wife.

She was willing to go the extra mile. She not only offered Eliezer water to drink but brought water up the steps of the well to feed 10 animals which had the most voracious of water appetite; camels. It is one thing to feed a man but to feed a camel, now that is something else. That was some kind of woman.

She moved with haste to solve an unannounced problem. Oh to find a wife that moves with haste to solve problems. Never marry a problem creator, always seek a problem solver.

She was designed with everything that he would need to finish his assignment. Powerful! Brothers, make sure the wife you choose has what you need in order for you to grow into a better man and become what you were called to become.

Eliezer held his peace until she had done the entire task that he had asked the Lord for her to do. He was a patient man but sometimes we are impatient when it comes to choosing a spouse. Sometimes a temporary comes dressed in permanent clothing. Wait on the Lord because she will be worth it.

Psalms 16:11

"You will show me the path of life; in Your presence is fullness of joy, at Your right hand there are pleasures forevermore" Psalms 16:11 (Amplified Bible, 1987). Brothers, I want to let you know that God knows how to produce joy and pleasures in a marriage. Who do you think invented marriage and sex? God did, but to enjoy them both you have to bring Him (God) into the marriage relationship. They are in His presence and at His right hand.

Over the years, some have attempted to distort what were intended to be a tremendous benefit to everyone (marriage and sex). This distortion is a diabolical deviation from what was intended to bless both the man and the woman. It's time to love right and get the fullness of joy back into our marriages.

Relationship Killers

Some relationship killers are activated before you begin a relationship and others while you are in the middle of a relationship. Some are the same for male and female and some are specific to one or the other. Either way they are designed to end or at least maim the relationship or marriage so that it will not complete its purpose. Let us look at 6 that are common to both male and female, the last 3 being more common to the man.

Unforgiveness: It is big and it is vitally important in order to be a healthy person and to have a healthy relationship. It can eat away at your soul, hinder your physical health and unhinge your heart from the success designed for it. True forgiveness does not ask you to forget but it does ask you to release people from what they have done to you or others. It does you no good to hold forgiveness from others as this does nothing to help them or yourself. Would you like to sleep better at night? How about keeping your blood pressure down? Why not bypass strokes and aneurisms? Jesus was a forgiver even at the point of being murdered. Who have you forgiven lately?

Degrading Speech: It's not funny to put down someone by calling them outside of their names in a degrading way. I used to be like that, especially in school where I could make people cry with my words. I represented my initials very well at that time. I have my mouth under much greater control now, blessing and not cursing, and I am ever striving to see the fruit of the Book of James 3:2, **"For we all often stumble and fall and offend in many things. And if anyone does not offend in speech (never says the wrong things) he is a fully developed character and a perfect man, able to control his whole body and to curb his entire nature"** (Amplified Bible, 1987).

Thank God for those of you that are able to say the right things all the time but for those of us that are still growing into that level, we strive to speak the right words so that we do not kill any more good relationships in our lives. It is hard enough to get a good relationship going, and then to kill it with the wrong words is truly disheartening.

Lying: Women can read through a lie like Perry Mason in a courtroom. (Ask your parents who Perry Mason is). They pay attention to detail and human beings are creatures of habit. As men, you usually do the same thing given the same circumstance. They have been studying you from day one and if you have told a lie one time it will be recorded and processed. Most of the time, the second lie will verify your lying behavior. Do you blink more frequently? Do you begin to stutter? Do your palms sweat? Brothers, she already knows. So to avoid killing a good relationship, tell the truth, even if it hurts you.

Ignoring her needs: This is so not a good practice for a man but especially a husband. A woman needs that attention and appreciation. She dresses for you, she puts on a particular perfume for you, she walks a certain way for you, she smiles for you, she cooks just for you, she takes care of the home for you, she prays for you, she sacrifices for you, she rests her body for you, she ignores others for you, she endures stuff just for you, she foregoes a lot for you, she helps you to be who you must be and so much more. The least that you can do is to be thankful and appreciative for all that she does for you. Never let another man compliment your wife more than you do.

She also needs affection. They are built for affection. From her skin to her heart to the deepest recesses of her being, she is interconnected with all types of neurons and transmitters that flow together like tributaries connecting to the Amazon. Yes, she is an Amazon woman if you can get the tributaries flowing in the right way by applying the right affection.

Insulting her: This is one that I cannot stand to see men do in public, and if it happens in the public eye, then it is obvious they do it in private. To insult comes from a Latin word which means to jump on and that is exactly what you are doing when you insult your woman or your wife. You are jumping on her. It would be the same thing if you did it to her physically.

How would you like it if every time you were in public and tried to engage in a conversation some man just jumped on you? It would not be fun right? You would not be excited to be around that guy and you just might end up in jail because of his behavior. Try that exercise. Get a person that you know fairly well to literally jump on you during a public conversation with others. Now you know how she feels. You can kill a good relationship with bad behavior.

Belittling her views: To belittle her views is to commit relationship suicide. Women are built to see perspectives you cannot see even if it is right in front of you. They use both sides of their brains at the same time while men hardly ever do. By the time she gives you her view she has anticipated your response and formulated the next level of action. If you try the old adage that you are the man of the house and what you say goes, then you are signing the death warrant for the relationship, not to mention setting yourself up for a cold bed (or couch).

It goes back to value, what value do you place on her? Is she valuable as a friend, partner, confidant, lifetime lover, or only your cook, cleaner and child bearer? Realize that God has blessed you way beyond what you deserve with a good wife and an awesome marriage. Because of this, constantly raise the value you place on her opinions. Loving her this way is right and it breeds life into the relationship. Don't kill it!

The Washing Machine has 2 Cycles

As a side note to these Relationship Killers I wanted to give you some advice that will help you to have great relationships that will never truly die. Read the Book of Proverbs 18:20-21 with me, "**A man's [moral] self shall be filled with the fruit of his mouth; and with the consequence of his words he must be satisfied [whether good or evil]. Death and life are in the power of the tongue, and they who indulge in it shall eat the fruit of it [for death or life]**" (Amplified Bible, 1987). Notice that many of *the relationship killers* and the *qualities to look for in a wife* come clothed in your words. Yes my brothers, your words (and hers also) do the most good or the most harm to your relationship.

You will turn on 2 cycles with the power of your tongue; the life cycle and the death cycle. The obvious choice, if offered, will be to turn on the life cycle. This is why your mouth is like a washing machine with 2 cycles. To be the best husband that you can be you must be a man that is working on turning on the life cycle for the woman in your life with every waking moment. Wash her with your words and keep the life cycle on.

The verse begins with letting you know that you will be filled with the fruit of your mouth. In other words, the seeds you plant today will be the fruit you eat tomorrow and you choose whether or not it is good or evil fruit. Not God, not your friends, not your family, not the government but only you. You feed yourself death or life every 86,400 seconds that God gives you to live daily. Some men waste great relationships by switching on the wrong cycle. Don't do it. Even if you are going to end a relationship, you can still be a class act and not turn on the death cycle against her. Remember, you will eat the fruit of it later on no matter who you wash with it.

Qualities to look for in a wife

*She will **submit** to your leadership and love as the Church submits to the leadership and love of Christ.* Ephesians 5:22-24. Do you want her to submit? Then show her that you will do anything to satisfy her the right way. Do you want to be the head? Then give her something to look up to. Do you want her to respect you? Then produce the behavior that attracts respect. Do you want her to honor you? Then position yourself for honor by doing honorable things. Do you want to be the leader? Then give her something to follow. A virtuous agaphilerosa will not mind submitting to you then.

Your leadership style, young man, is simply a leadership style of love. To submit is a military term. In a God ordained marriage the husband and the wife are like generals in their respective branches of the military and God is the Commander in Chief. The husband is neither greater than the wife nor is the wife greater than the husband. They have different titles and separate duties but one Supreme Leader. When they go to battle an enemy they must submit to each other's leadership or else there will be chaos and loss.

Can you picture the USA military force in disarray because the general of the Air Force does not want to submit to the General of the Army and vice versa? Submit to each other the right way and win. Be selfish, do your own thing and lose. Submission to each other is the right way to love.

*She will be in **agreement** with you for your purpose as it relates to where the relationship is heading.* Amos 3:3. Do not seek a woman who wants to move you out of your purpose into weakness. Seek a wife who will help you into your purpose which is your strength. Remember Samson and Delilah? Delilah's name means *feeble* and she made Samson feeble and weak. Remember Jezebel and Ahab? Jezebel's name means *Baal is boss* and she became the boss of Ahab, her husband and king. Her name also means incite. Her *insight* was how to *incite* her husband out of God's will for his life.

As a husband, you want your wife to be in agreement with you according to purpose. Therefore, it is necessary for a man to have his purpose already known and stipulated so that she has something to agree to. That means that you will have to spend some quality time with God for that revelation to get to you. If not, seek wise counsel about your purpose from a mentor who may be able to see what you cannot see in yourself.

*She will have or would want to have a **sensitive** ear to the voice of God.* Luke 1:26-38. I certainly can appreciate a wife with the ability to hear from God. During my marriage to Jessy and even before we were married, there were those times that I knew she had heard from the Lord. One time in particular was at Youth Camp in Toco, Trinidad. We had a long talk one night where I expressed to her how I truly felt and by the time the night was over she had said that she would pray about it/me.

The next morning she was a different person. Came to find out that she did pray and the Lord touched her in a special way while she slept and she said that she woke up a different person, anxious to see me that morning. Isn't it great when God does spiritual surgery on someone while they are sleeping and it benefits both of you? Keep doing it Dr. Jesus.

The rest is our story but brothers, suffice it to say, you need this in your life. A woman who hears the Lord, who can find? For her price is far above precious jewels and anything money can buy. She will become so valuable to you that you will never want to be without her.

She will be a **help** suited to the vision that you have. Genesis 2:18, 22. Eve was built up and made into a woman by God specifically for Adam. Brothers, I suggest you hold off marriage proposal until you can verify that your lady was built up and made especially for you by God. God will give you purpose because He will call you to something. Whatever He calls you to will need help and you will need help. The wife that He has for you will be perfectly suited to help you carry out His call that is upon your life.

I am not speaking about a call of God to be a pastor or a preacher. God does not call everyone to be a pastor, but He does call everyone to be something. Maybe your call will be to become a teacher or an engineer or a pilot but whatever you are called to, she will be suited just for that. I often say that if God called you to the ocean He will not give you a spouse that loves the desert.

She will **connect** to your innermost being when she speaks because she belongs there. Genesis 2:21-23. There has to be some chemistry involved here. God is the glue to make this bond work because He was the doctor that applied the amnesia for Adam to sleep and then surgically, spiritually and physically removed a part of him from which He created Eve. Believe me when I say that it is a beautiful thing when your wife speaks and you hear her all the way down inside. Do you know how that happens? It is because she was already there. This is not her first rodeo with you. The master designer formed her with parts of your DNA spiritually speaking and when she speaks it will be like you have known each other for the longest time, for a lifetime even.

As a matter of fact, you both will become so connected that your thoughts will begin to line up together, you will finish each other sentences, you will desire some similar things and eventually may even begin to look and act similar to each other (rare but it exists). Seriously though, listen to what she says when she speaks. Her voice will penetrate the blocks and locks that you have placed on your heart. Let her speak.

*She will be willing to risk everything to **follow** the instructions of the Holy Spirit.* Luke 1:38. I am not talking about a "spooky" person but rather one that is sensitive to the leading of the Holy Spirit and is willing to obey Him. Mary was not voted "Most likely to win the Miss Israel 3 BC Beauty Pageant" but she was chosen by God to carry our Lord and Savior Jesus the Christ. What an honor!

Agaphilerosos, of all the things that you will need in a wife, in your agaphilerosa, the ability to hear from God and respond will be one of the most crucial. This is my personal opinion. Mary was a woman that could hear from God and respond. Make sure that you do not miss out on this key aspect of your Agaphilerosa. Why? Because many people hear from God but few follow His instructions. Many are called but few are chosen. The chosen follow. If she does not want to follow His instructions she most likely will not want to follow yours.

*The Lord will **design, prepare and preserve** a wife for you and not hide her from you.* Genesis 2:21. Proverbs 18:22. When you do find your wife she will be a good God thing as the Book of Proverbs mentioned here refers to her as. The word "thing" however, was added by the privilege of the translators and may conjure up the wrong image. It really can be read, "Whosoever finds a wife **finds good** and obtains **favor** from the Lord." To amplify it even further let us look at 3 of the words used in the original text; let us explore some of the possibilities of the Old Testament (OT) Hebrew language in this verse.

Finds: To secure, to acquire, to get a thing sought, to encounter, to learn, to fall in with, to hit like a jackpot (not a punching bag), to be in the possession of, and to attain to, are some of the expressions of the word "matsa" in the OT Hebrew language.

Good: "Towb" in the OT Hebrew language means pleasant and agreeable to the senses, pleasant to the higher nature, excellent of its kind, valuable in estimation, happiness and prosperity of man's sensuous nature, and bounty.

Favor: "Ratsown" in the OT Hebrew language means goodwill, favor, acceptance, desire, will, pleasure and delight.

Brothers, you can rewrite that verse of scripture in a myriad of ways and it will always come out with a blessing attached to it. Imagine now that God has designed, prepared and preserved your wife, one exactly like this, just for you. Is that love or is that love? I believe that it is the best thing that could ever happen to you because a wife that brings these things into your life just has to be. Is it any wonder that happily married and purposely living husbands and wives tend to live longer, increase income, possess better health, have a more stable family, serve others at a higher level and overall enjoy life?

On the other hand, is it any wonder that the enemy of our lives, satanas himself or the devil, attacked the first marriage and continues to release things into the earth that attack marriages today? He does not like you or your Eden, that place that God has for you in this life. He will do everything in his power to stop you from having a purposeful marriage and to keep you from loving the right way.

He will create industries designed to keep you from understanding that God has preserved a great life for you and it is in your marriage. He will want you to stay single and sow your *wild oats,* and later on as you wrap up your life you will discover that you are sexually stimulated but psychologically empty and spiritually dead. Brother, get over yourself and begin to seek what has been designed, prepared and preserved for you. Your greatest and best life resides within the confines of a God ordained marriage. Trust me, I know this.

Grace Nuggets

As I wrap up this important Movement I would like to leave some parting words with you my brothers. It is the same words that I gave to the ladies but tailored just for you.

A real man has a Leadership style of Love and will never force submission out of his wife. If submission is forced then it is a master/slave or an owner/worker relationship. Earn it like Jesus did. If however she does not want that style of leadership before marriage, then you should probably move on. Your choice.

In true love, agreement does not come before advantage. Jesus demonstrated His love for us by giving us the advantage first. We then agree with Him for what He has done and then seek to do the same for Him. Become a man that loves to give the advantage and you will attract a lady that loves to do the same. Giving the advantage is the pinnacle of selflessness and the antithesis or the direct opposite of selfishness.

There is a dilemma that most men face and it is this; should I choose a wife with my physical eyes or with my spiritual eyes? Let me help you. Being selfless is always better than being selfish or self-more. Always choose every day to serve God and others through selflessness. Why?

Because your self-effort will cause you to choose what you think is best for you which is the person who can give the most to you. But the grace of God will cause you to possess what is best for you which is the person who can receive the most from you. It is in this position that you will begin to receive more than you could have ever imagined from the person that you freely gave all that you could. God will not give you someone to hurt you; He will give you someone to help you.

The Lord has already gone ahead of you and has chosen your Rebecca. The Holy Spirit has anointed her to bring comfort into your life and everything else that you need. Remove the limits you may have placed upon God the Father and see how He can give you someone that you do not even think you deserve.

What are the limits you ask? Where is she, when will you meet, what is her race, her age, her education, her social status, and things of that nature. I learned much of that lesson with Jessy. Now the limits are off and I live the limitless life.

To the married kings and brothers who may be struggling in their marriage right now, there is so much you can glean in these pages to help steady your ship and prepare you to arrive at your destination. You may not have to get a divorce from your wife, you may just need to divorce yourself from selfishness and take the limits off of God. Loving her is right and you do not want to be wrong about it.

Take Aways M6

- ✓ Husbands are managers and therefore they manage. Husbands are leaders and therefore they lead.

- ✓ The Greek version of the word "husband" from the Love Manual said that a husband is how you distinguish an adult man from a boy.

- ✓ Brothers, "boy" tendencies have to die off so that husband behaviours can show up.

- ✓ While a manager handles the operation of a thing, the leader cuts the path for its progress. The success for the operation of marriage today is in the hands of the manager but the vision that produced it and sees its future purpose is in the heart of the leader.

- ✓ Hanging up the shoes takes place beforehand and that shows God that you are ready to handle a wife. Boys play around with temporaries but husbands build around a permanent.

- ✓ You manage with passion, you lead with vision, and you operate with compassion because you are teachable, reachable and reliable.

- ✓ Brothers, here is the reason why you must be teachable. If nobody can tell you anything then eventually you will have nobody to tell anything to.

- ✓ God cannot fellowship with you as a leader if He cannot reach you as a student.

- ✓ Become reliable: dependable, trustworthy and honest. Never lose those qualities, they are what great husbands and marriages are made of.

- ✓ When a man is married he is technically born again into a relationship that he has never been in before and so must look to cut the old umbilical cords that cannot sustain him in his new environment.

- ✓ That which nourished him in the old relationship cannot nourish him in the new relationship.

- ✓ In order to love her the right way in the garden she must be the right one for you. To try to love the wrong one in a right way is to risk forfeiting the purpose for which your marriage was created. What God has joined together has purpose.

- ✓ You will not have to eat from another man's garden if you feed yourself properly from your own. Wise men learn how to cultivate the fruit that is in their own garden and not waste time cultivating someone else's fruit tree.

- ✓ As a husband you should never leave home thirsty because you may end up at someone else's river trying to satisfy a thirst that should be quenched in your own garden by your own rivers.

- ✓ Not only that, but you want a wife that can see your wealth in you and knows how to help you get it out into the earth. A marriage is not about being broke together; it's about being rich together.

- ✓ Don't let a temporary use you to blow resources, rather use resources to bless your permanent.

- ✓ What you need to be alive and to live long and prosper is planted within the marriage that God placed you in.

- ✓ You are designed to be a life giver and a life receiver.

- ✓ Things that are alive communicate. That is why it is imperative to choose a wife who communicates well, who can communicate life and not just talk.

- ✓ A good wife is someone who will never leave you hungry, thirsty, poor or dead.

- ✓ Your obedience to what God says will protect you from disaster and determine your success in the marriage relationship.

- ✓ Deception will dismantle God's design for your marriage leaving you as a statistic of failure wondering what happened.

- ✓ The tree of the knowledge of good and evil is less about God restricting you and more about God protecting you.

- ✓ The word of God is first and is necessary for all the things we build and for everything we believe including choosing a spouse and having a God ordained marriage.

- ✓ Good husbands are great givers.

- ✓ Walk in the blessings of obedience and you will not fulfil the disobedience that brings the curse.

- ✓ Never marry a problem creator, always seek a problem solver.

- ✓ Sometimes a temporary comes dressed in permanent clothing. Wait on the Lord.

- ✓ Relationship killers are designed to end or at least maim the relationship to keep it from completing its purpose.

- ✓ They have been studying you from day one and if you have told a lie one time it will be recorded and processed.

- ✓ Never let another man compliment your wife more than you do.

- ✓ In other words, the seeds you plant today will be the fruit you eat tomorrow and you choose whether or not it is good or evil fruit.

- ✓ Submit to each other the right way and win. Be selfish, do your own thing and lose. Submission to each other is the right way to love.

- ✓ Do not seek a woman who wants to move you out of your purpose into weakness. Seek a wife who will help you into your purpose which is your strength.

- ✓ Brothers, I suggest you hold off marriage proposal until you can verify that your lady was built up and made especially for you by God.

- ✓ God does not call everyone to be a pastor, but He does call everyone to be something.

- ✓ Many are called but few are chosen. The chosen follow. If she does not want to follow His instructions she most likely will not want to follow yours.

- ✓ Your enemy satanas will want you to stay single and sow your *wild oats,* and later on as you wrap up your life you will discover that you are sexually stimulated but psychologically empty and spiritually dead.

- ✓ God will not give you someone to hurt you; He will give you someone to help you.

- ✓ The limits are off! Live the limitless life.

- ✓ You may not have to get a divorce from your wife, you may just need to divorce yourself from selfishness and take the limits off of the God you serve. Loving her is right and you do not want to be wrong about it.

MOVEMENT 7

What things should you both have in common?

Move on from being a passive consumer of love to being a passionate conductor of love. Create some good love music with your spouse.

Quality versus Cheap

The both of you should be people of quality and not people who are cheap. Relationships exist on 1 spectrum with 2 opposite ends: quality and cheap. A person's character is set along the same spectrum. Every day you decide to be a person of quality or a cheap person. Every day you decide where you will stand on the spectrum. When I speak of quality I speak from the standpoint of the most quintessential relationship that can possibly exist or the most perfect embodiment of a Championship Relationship. It is the epitome of excellence. In a quality marriage each person tends to the needs of the other to the best of their ability. They see the other person's need as more important than their own and the feeling is reciprocated.

When I speak of cheap, I do not speak of a financial purchasing mindset necessarily. Cheap, where your relationship is concerned, is more about how you view things in the relationship than anything else. A totally cheap person sees themselves as the sum total of the relationship and they are 100% vested in their own way. If two people are both 100% vested in their own selves then the relationship itself will be the cheapest it can be. It will not be any good. As my buddy, Pastor Brian said, "Cheap ting no good and good ting no cheap".

A cheap relationship has no lasting value. It is usually quick, fast and in a hurry. It is considered a quickie, always a quickie, nothing more than a quickie. Quality relationships have lasting value. They are usually long lasting selfless "other people centered" relationships.

Satisfaction is never compromised by speed. Cheap focuses on as fast as possible but quality focuses on as long as possible. Cheap wants to be there by the next breath but quality wants to be there until the last breath. Cheap will use any old material to build fast but quality will use strong materials to build to last.

For those who chose to get involved in "one-night stands" or "one-hour stands", they have chosen the cheapest and quickest way to get their lust desires met. Those who choose that life style will bear the scars of low quality living until they make a decision to change. Things produced out of a cheap relationship cost you more later on. The statistics are out there and you can find them if you choose to. Families built around cheap relationships often have the most hardships, suffer the most consequences, and pay the highest price imaginable.

Some statistics even reveal that things like elevated high school drop-out rates, criminal activity, incarcerations, promiscuous behavior, child pregnancies, violent acts (especially by men), and more are a result of cheap people in cheap relationships. Yes beloved, cheap today is expensive tomorrow.

Imagine if you will, you visit a furniture store and see a table that you like that will be perfect for your large TV. It is well made and of a high quality. The price is $500 but you do not have all of it at that moment. You want it, but now you have to wait.

On the way home you pass by a yard sale and see a cheap table that cost $5. It is big enough but you can see the material is far inferior to the one from the store. The table in the yard sale was used by someone for many years and then put out in exchange for cash. You start to convince yourself that it can work. I cannot say this point enough. *You convince yourself* that the $5 table can do the job of the $500 table. You think that you have found a deal at a bargain price and it *must* be God's will for you. By the way, some cheap purchases may have no back up support, may come without warranty and can be final. Be careful what you purchase when the price is very low. You may have no recourse after purchase.

After you bring home the $5 table you stand back looking at it and sense that it may not hold out for long. But again, you convince yourself that it can work, for now. Maybe you just need to give it a try. You can change parts of it if you need to. Your family and friends tell you that it looks a bit unsafe yet you press on because you have convinced yourself that it can work.

It does! It works for all of a day and then it breaks down and your new TV goes tumbling down like Humpty Dumpty. You have a mess on your hand because you convinced yourself that cheap was the way to go. Now you have to get money for a new TV and you still are in need of a good quality table.

Beloved, cheap is never the way to go in your relationships. You can recover from a broken table and a broken TV but it may take you a long time to deal with a cheap relationship when it breaks. Cheap people usually break down just after you bring them into your life. They will not work, they will not make the necessary personal sacrifices and they will not initiate the changes necessary for a successful relationship. They will not give you their 3 most important commodities: time, resources and energy.

They will surely add little to no value to you and will actually begin to bring down your personal value. They often try to make you do things you never thought that you would do, sometimes by force. Why do you think that they are on the side of the road? Their last owner does not want them anymore. Hello! If someone discards something that is cheap, why would you even think about investing *your* commodities to bring it into your life? Check yourself!

Characteristics of Quality People and their Relationships

Quality people and their relationships show up looking to see what they can give and not what they can get. When quality people and their relationships show up in your life they will have a desire to give to you whatever they can provide. They are often drawn to you because of your need knowing that they have the supply needed to make you better. That is quality love.

When a person or a couple comes to you and is constantly trying to get things from you that is not love that is called lust. It is a by-product of selfishness. Lust is cheap, easy and more prevalent today than ever before. Many are programmed to take the cheap and easy path and this programming comes through the media; it comes through mediocre parenting; it comes from adults that do not care about quality; it comes through friends that are cheap and the list goes on and on. When you are taught that the right choice is hard and the wrong choice is easy, what kind of mentally do you think you will develop? Cheap material is easier to handle and easier to manipulate but it is never satisfied.

Quality people and their relationships will work,

sacrifice and change in order to help their counterpart to become all that God has called them to become. Jesus did just that for all of us. He did the work the Father asked of Him. He went to the cross and He gave His all so that we can have all that we need to become all that we are supposed to be. If He did that for you how much more should you do for your spouse? It is time to do the work, make the personal sacrifices and initiate the changes necessary for a quality relationship.

In addition, as a couple, your relationship should be one of influence to those in your circle to motivate them to reach higher, go farther and accomplish more than they have ever done. Quality does not settle for mediocre even if it seems to be the most common choice available. Rather, quality will have a pep talk with itself and create avenues to assist others into success, no matter the cost. Quality never wants to leave you cheap, never.

Quality people and their relationships will attract quality people and relationships. When you decide to be a person of quality and you begin to build a quality relationship with another quality person, other quality relationships will find you. Observe couples who are selfless with each other. Notice that they hang out with other couples who are also like that. They just seem to find each other. Also, if you have had cheap relationships in the past and then participated in a quality relationship it will be increasingly difficult to return to a cheap way of relating.

Just as quality attracts quality so does cheap attract cheap. Notice people who are selfish and see how many relationships they go through in a year. Look at who they hang out with, who they pursue and who they attract. It is human nature to flow with your kind and so they stick together.

It has been said that opposites attract. That may be true in the laboratory of science but not so much in the laboratory of life. Remember the "Odd Couple", Oscar and Felix? Can you imagine the stress that can be brought into a marriage if the couple were like they were? One is clean and the other is dirty. One cares about others and the other does not.

What if you like going to the gym, getting on the bench with barbell in hand but your spouse prefers getting on the couch with a beer in hand? Beloved, you may look for someone that is your opposite if you want to but as for me and my future wife, we will be looking for quality. There is even a text in the Love Manual that warns us against being unequally yoked together with unbelievers (in every aspect, including quality).

In the Book of 2 Corinthians 6:14 it says, **"Do not be unequally yoked with unbelievers [do not make mismated alliances with them or come under a different yoke with them, inconsistent with your faith]. For what partnership have right living and right standing with God with iniquity and lawlessness? Or how can light have fellowship with darkness?"** (Amplified Bible, 1987). How can quality have intimate fellowship with cheap? If your faith is for quality then by all means expect to attract some quality into your life.

Do not grow your faith in other areas and then have depleted faith when it comes to choosing a spouse. That would be cheap.

Quality people and their relationships will impact cheap people in such a way that they too will want to become someone of quality. We are all born with the nature of cheap and with the potential of quality buried within us. One is entangled in what we call our flesh and the other is embedded within what we call our spirit. The one that we feed will dominate the one that we starve.

When I first met Jessy I had already encountered quality people and I had that lingering feeling that I could have more than cheap relationships if I worked, sacrificed and changed. To get with Jessy I knew I could not remain cheap; my quality level had to be stepped up. Fortunately for me she gave me time to get up there. Now I could never return to cheap relationships. I have become, and I want to remain a person of quality.

With every thought, every word and every action you must feed the quality seed within you in order to become what you were designed to be; an ambassador of quality. God did not design you for cheap relationships, He designed you for quality relationships. He placed that quality seed within you. He did His part and now it is your turn to feed the seed. I suggest that you cease feeding any cheap seeds that show up. Instead, make a mark in a cheap person's life today that will never be erased by showing them what quality looks like. Question, what did you feed today? Represent your designer well today.

Quality people and their relationships are blessed because they have a purpose and a destination. Whenever I am conducting an Agaphileros Intimate Moments session I tell couples to name their relationship. Why? When you name something you give it an identity, a characteristic, a nature as it were. Why do we name our babies? Why do we name our vehicles? Why do we name our teams? With a name also comes purpose. The purpose connects you to your God given T.A.G.S. (talents, abilities, gifts, skills). Great people will always talk about purpose with you and they will push you out of your comfort zone. Like a ship, the design will make the destination an obvious choice. Where is your relationship heading to?

I truly believe that marriages are purposed based. As a matter of fact, God does not do anything without a purpose. He is the most purposeful being. Whether it is God bringing Abraham and Sarah together or Isaac and Rebekah together, God is always planning ahead. He was getting the lineage of Jesus ready and He is doing the same thing with you. Destination Jesus! That is why He has me talking about quality relationships with you right now. The shift is on for you. Destination, Championship Relationship!

I want to interject a confession right here that pertains to us being people of quality. No matter who you are or where you are, I want you to speak this confession loudly. Hear yourself speaking these words.

Confession of Quality

I am a person of quality and I am not a cheap person. I think quality thoughts about my relationships therefore when thoughts come to my mind about my relationships I choose the thoughts of quality and reject the thoughts that are cheap. I speak quality words about my relationships therefore when words come to my mouth concerning my relationships I choose the words of quality and reject the words that are cheap. I perform quality actions for my relationships every day in every way and I reject the actions that are cheap. I am not ashamed of being a person of quality therefore I promote quality in every area of my character. I enter every relationship to see what I can give to the other person, I will help them to become who God has called them to be, I attract quality people around me, I influence others to become people of quality and every relationship that I am involved in has a purpose and a God-given destination. I will continue to do the necessary work, make the personal sacrifices and initiate the selfless changes in order to grow in my disposition of quality, thereby making all my relationships quality relationships. I am quality!

We have a Champion: Love!

Love is the highest quality material that you can use to build a Championship Relationship. Love is God's championship material. If you were to verify what is the deepest part of the ocean you will find that the *Mariana Trench* is the champion. If you were to research what is the highest mountain on earth you will find that *Mount Everest* is the champion. Well likewise, when you research what is the greatest building tool that a person can use to build a relationship, we have a champion. It is *Love!*

A champion is better than everybody else. A champion is one who has been tested and tried, and have come out on top of the list. Love conquers all, it never fails and it never loses. It is undefeated in every relationship that it has entered. Even when you think that it is going down for the count, love is going to bounce back. People of quality build relationships with love material.

Beloved, if you build anything with cheap materials it will eventually collapse. There is only so much duct tape in the world. Broken relationships come about because cheap people use cheap materials to build cheap relationships. If you look over your life and see a string of broken relationships then you can tell that cheap was there. All that you have to do is look for brokenness and you will find cheap. Get the champion back in the game.

8 Foundational Principles of an Agaphileros Marriage

Beloved, here are 8 suggestions that I want to give to you if you are endeavoring to have an Agaphileros Marriage. 8 is the number of new beginnings and if you are in a season of marriage turmoil, grab a hold of these foundational principles and build your marriage again. If you are engaged or seeing someone who you would like to get married to, by all means use what you can before the big day. Chances are that if they do not want an Agaphileros type marriage your "ship" will be tossed about more than it has to be. If you are unmarried, this is great information that you can begin to develop within yourself so that you will be successful in marriage when it comes along. Either way, this 8's for you.

1. *There should be **one** vision for the marriage.* Someone may ask, "Why can't we have two visions in the marriage? Why can't I have a vision for my life and my spouse have a vision for their own? Surely God can handle that. As long as we love each other, nothing else should matter, right?"

Beloved, I can only advise you based on what I know. This is what Proverbs 29:18 says. **"Where there is no vision [no redemptive revelation of God], the people perish; but he who keeps the law [of God, which includes that of man] – blessed (happy, fortunate, and enviable) is he"** (Amplified Bible, 1987). It says a lot does it not? Notice with me a couple of things.

It does not say visions, it says *vision*. A vision can be an act or power of anticipating that which will or may come to be, (Dictionary.com, 2014). When God brings a man and a woman together, it is with the intent to make them see as one, to have one vision. One vision can have complimentary parts to it but it is still one vision.

Follow me closely beloved. When God brought Adam and Eve together, they had their vision of what He intended for them (instructions from Him). If they did what He asked them to do then they would have what He had promised to them. The moment they introduced a new and separate vision, there was failure. The new vision was an opposing and deceptive vision. The new vision was the antithesis of what God (love) had ordained for them.

God gave them the vision of what they were to work on to become who He made them to be. Once Eve allowed a secondary and opposing vision into the marriage, and Adam signed off on it, the end of God's vision was inevitable. When God's vision for your marriage or relationship has to compete with another vision, di-vision eventually shows up. I believe di-vision is really die-vision because a great marriage cannot sustain two opposing visions. When there are two opposing visions, one will eventually die.

Once Eve anticipated something *other* than what God said, what God said began to die in the womb of her spirit. Her flesh came alive and Adam sealed the destruction with his support of another vision. The process of die-vision had begun.

Think about a failed marriage. When does it begin to

fail? More often than not, it begins to fail when one or both persons introduce another vision (that which will be), into their lives and by default into their marriage. I urge you to come together in agreement under one vision for the marriage, especially before you say, "I do". It will help you to stay on track with what God has intended for the marriage.

2. *There should be **mutual submission** to one another in the fear of the Lord.* The Book of Ephesians 5:21 says, **"Be subject to one another out of reverence for Christ (the Messiah, the Anointed One)"** (Amplified Bible, 1987). Submitting to each other is as if you are reverencing or paying high respect to Christ himself. It is basically serving and Jesus himself talked about serving as being the highest form of greatness. Serving your spouse is not a chore, it is a privilege. The world will tell you the opposite and make you believe that when you are great others must serve you, even your spouse. It's time to love right beloved. Those who serve are great in the eyes of God.

Mutual submission reveals the level of reverence that you have for Christ in your marriage. Reverencing Christ is submitting to the anointing that is upon Him to do what He does. Submitting to your spouse is submitting to the anointing that is upon their lives that enables them to do what they do. No big "I's" and little "you's" in marriage. The Book of 1 Corinthians 7 also touches on this subject by letting you know that your body belongs to your spouse and vice versa. Mutuality! You are supposed to mutually submit your bodies to one another on your wedding day and thereafter.

3. *You both should **leave** other relationships to make this one the **most important** one.* The Book of Genesis 2:24 says, **"Therefore a man shall leave his father and mother and shall become united and cleave to his wife, and they shall become one flesh"** (Amplified Bible, 1987). Adam mentions father and mother without even having a physical father and mother. He did not have buddies or pals. Eve did not have girlfriends and BFFs who she hung out with. Yet the

words recorded are so poignant, especially today. Those words may have been added by the Holy Spirit to help men especially. The wives that God has preserved for us as men are wives that will connect to us within and without. They will be specifically designed by God to help us into the destiny for our lives.

Most likely, the vision for the marriage will already be within the man. The wife will be designed to help articulate and fine tune that which God has birthed in her husband. Notice, the vision that Adam possessed was implanted in him by God. Eve was already planted into Adam at the time the vision was being birthed. She has the substance of that vision already in her because she was in the same place where the vision was and both she and the vision came from God. She is familiar with it which is why sometimes your wife can see what you are capable of even when you cannot see it. So Adam, your job is to leave and cleave. She has been in you, but now you both must be in each other. Your purpose depends on it.

Another important thing about leaving and cleaving is that you both must be willing to build a new world with some new relationships. I know I touched on it before but it is worth touching on again. Certainly you each had separate worlds before you met, but once you cross over into marriage, you cannot bring everyone from your old world into your new world.

And do not bring your spouse into your world and expect them to adjust. That again is selfishness. That is why it is called marriage and not carriage, marry not carry. To marry is to create a new covenant, a new relationship, one that never existed before. To carry is to take something with you that you have the option to leave anywhere and anytime. To leave is to not carry something. Do not carry your father and mother's old into your new. Your parents had you in their world but now it is time for both of you to build a new one.

There may have been some foundational principles that your parents had and if it is worthy of transference into your new world by all means take that with you. By the way, you both should agree on what comes along. Build a better world than what your parents had, depending on the Holy Spirit for help.

Beloved, you cannot carry *all* of the old into the new because sometimes that carriage may lead to carnage. She is not your momma and he is not your daddy. Even a mother-in-law, a father-in-law, family members and friends can break down what you are trying to build up. Old boyfriends, girlfriends and exes are notorious for dismantling new relationships. When you speak with each other about the new world you must come into agreement about this. Do not make Harry pay for what Barry did and do not let Shirley pay for the sins of Shelley. Build something new and keep the drama out of it.

Another thing beloved, weigh and balance all expert advice that you encounter by the principal scale which is the Love Manual. Just because someone has a Dr. preceding their name or hosts a show or calls themselves a coach does not mean they will always speak what is best for your new world. Most of them are practicing their profession just like I am but the Love Manual is not practicing anything. It has proven itself through every generation. Whatever I say or someone else says about relationships, weigh it against the Love Manual.

4. *Neither one of you must want to bring* **shame** *to the relationship or to each other.* The Book of Genesis 2:25 says, **"And the man and his wife were both naked and were not embarrassed or ashamed in each other's presence"** (Amplified Bible, 1987). So often in marriages and in relationships overall, human nature pushes you to protect yourself and your feelings. Adam and Eve were in the middle of God's vision for their marriage, they were serving one another, they were building a new world and life was grand.

They were naked and open before one another without any shame.

However, I do not think that this text is only referring to the physical since they were clothed in some type of glorious covering. They were transparent with each other. Marriage is not some shadowy covenant. Marriage must be transparent before it can eradicate shame. Transparency brings clarity. If you are ashamed of someone's past then do not build a future with them. What you are ashamed of today will come up in a conversation or disagreement tomorrow. Unresolved shame is like cancer cells just waiting for the right opportunity to grow into something deadly.

That describes the shame of the past. But the text can also refer to "shame" of the future. Keeping shame away from your marriage should be on the forefront of everything you do because if you do the wrong thing as an individual, shame can descend faster than a speeding bullet upon your marriage.

Have you ever seen those live press conferences when some politician, business leader or famous person has to explain their infidelity? In today's world, millions can see them through the lens of one camera. As they confess their faults their spouses stand by their side. The masses are not just looking at the offender; they are also looking at the spouse, trying to ascertain their emotional state in the midst of the shame. Beloved, avoid all of that by resisting the opportunity to bring shame to your spouse, children, and everyone else that is connected to you. That is why you need the Holy Spirit and the Love Manual. Don't leave home without them.

The Holy Spirit will lead and guide you into truth and away from deception. He will intercede for you when you don't know what to pray for. He will teach you how to love right and how to stay away from loving the wrong way. He will emancipate your mind from the mental slavery of selfishness and free you into selflessness. By the time He is finished working with you, your spouse will be in awe. Never underestimate the power of the Holy Spirit to keep you away from shame when you give in to His leadership.

The Love Manual will be your scale, your wisdom, your textbook, your workbook, your play book, your love book, your driver's manual, your knowledge manual, your corrective action manual, your verification department, your love library, your vision enhancer, your argument decider, and your "keep your behind away from that thing that will bring shame to your relationship" book. Today you can listen to it, read it and interact with it through many mediums. We really have no excuse.

5. *There should be a **desire** to **change** and the discipline to follow through.* Bishop TD Jakes said that people who are afraid of change are afraid of success (Jakes, 2014). Change is a prerequisite for success. Nothing happens unless something changes and a relationship does not become a championship relationship without both parties being willing to change. Changes within a relationship include adapting, evolving, adjusting and improving.

A desire is only as good as the discipline required to carry it all the way through to manifestation. Many people desire a good marriage but do not have the discipline needed to make their marriage become a good one. Many people desire to be healthier but lack the discipline necessary to make better health choices. Many people desire to start an enterprise but lack the discipline needed to get their business affairs in order.

People all over the world want to grow their income, obtain a better education, write a novel, be a world traveler, plant a garden, be a better parent, be a better son or daughter, be something more than they have ever been, but all too often they lack the discipline to turn their desire into reality.

One desire that a selfless person possesses is to continually change into a better person, and with that, to continue the never ending process of change until they breathe their last breath. There is just something about the husband or wife that continues to change into a better person that speaks of being a champion.

It is not only the characteristic of a championship spouse, but it is also the characteristic of all the leaders in the personal development arena. Change is their constant companion. Read the stories of people like Jim Rohn, Les Brown, John Maxwell and their counterparts and see what I mean. Read their books, listen to their recordings, engage their gift and see why change is their constant companion, and see why it should be yours as well.

Refusing to change or stopping the process of change is akin to giving up. The late great Sir Winston Churchill and the late great coach Jimmy Valvano said it best: Never give up! Real lovers, agaphileros lovers, keep changing and never give up changing. Your spouse may be content with your current improvements but you must not sit on your laurels, never be satisfied with your current levels. Keep changing to make your spouse even happier than before.

By the time you *learn* what the marriage covenant is all about, then *master* it and subsequently begin to *improve* it, you would have changed a whole lot about yourself. I am telling you with all sincerity, become a better agaphileros lover and you will look at yourself in the mirror and feel a sense of accomplishment and godly pride.

6. *There should be a desire to have a **fulfilling** relationship **designed** by God and lived by the both of you.* Think about what you would like your relationship to look like at the end of its journey. What will the epitaph of your relationship say? Will it say, "Here lays a relationship that was designed by God that was filled with enrichment, love and purpose," or will it say, "Here lays a relationship designed by two people that was filled with sorrow, missed opportunities and regret?"

Being fruitful will not always mean having children together because you may not, but it will always mean that the relationship will be fruitful in producing God's will in the earth.

Where you both live will be a better place because the both of you are there. There will be enrichment, there will be the feeling of love and there will be an accomplishing of purpose.

Nothing that God designs is for selfish gain. Let me say that again. Whatever God has joined together let not selfishness pull apart. There will not be a selfish purpose in an Agaphileros marriage. It will never be about just the two of you. God needs your marriage to emulate what true love is so that others can be blessed by it. You are supposed to be the examples of agaphileros; the way love is supposed to be.

The world desperately needs great examples of enriching, loving and purposeful relationships that bear great fruit. Others must want what you have; they must want that God kind of life that is rarely seen today. It is the God in you that will attract them.

Deep down inside, we all have a desire to have great fulfilling relationships. Even though at times good relationships fall apart, it is not because there is some design flaw that God placed in you. You can hang out with God every day and still screw up. Moses was in God's presence a lot yet got mad and struck the rock instead of honoring God by speaking to the rock. David was a man after God's own heart yet killed a man to get the man's wife. Abraham was the father of faith yet deceived others about who Sarah, his wife, was. Judas walked with Jesus yet betrayed him for 30 pieces of silver.

No beloved, the fault and the flaw is with us. We are the ones who place our own hands in the cookie jar or say the words we should not say or go to the places we should not go to. But do not let your own personal faults and flaws keep you from the pursuit of an agaphileros marriage. Other people are depending on the both of you to make it. Surely the road will be filled with challenges, and stumbling blocks will seemingly appear from nowhere, but you have all the equipment that you need to fulfill the purpose of your God designed relationship.

Here are 5 things to do in an agaphileros marriage. *Pray.* Converse with the master of relationships and the architect of true relationship success. *Read.* The Love manual is your greatest literary resource for relationship success. *Worship.* Nothing lifts a heavy burden like a good time of worship. *Praise.* Let it go with a shout and a Hallelujah. *Circle.* Stay connected to the people in your Go Team and your Grow Team. They are there to help you go through and grow through whatever you face.

    7. **Trust** *each other without recourse.* **Trust love**. Trust is big for any relationship, but in an agaphileros marriage it is paramount. Any great relationship will be built on trust because trust is a key component of love. We often say we trust God and since God is love we can actually say that we trust love. Yet have you ever considered that God trusts you? It may sound silly or even naïve but in reality, God trusts that you will take His mission for marriage and fulfill it in the earth. That is why He provided a virtuous woman for you, sir and a king for you, my lady.

    So if the great God Jehovah trusts you with this sacred covenant, should you not be able to trust each other also? Easier said than done, right? I know. Trust is hard to build up and easy to break down, yet it is necessary to win the championship.

    In essence, we build trust by what we say, and then by what we do about what we say. If I want you to trust me, then I must perform the actions that I have said that I will do in order to be a blessing to you. You in turn must do the same for me.

    To recourse is "to run back" as the original Latin suggests. Can a man or a woman run from God? Will a husband or a wife run from their marriage? Of course. Divorce has become so prevalent and marital betrayal so common-place that many people put certain exit strategies in place for the "just in case" events. This area can be a bit tricky because there are times that you must leave to save the lives of your family members, but more often than not, people enter marriages with exit strategies because they do not trust one another.

Things like a prenuptial agreement, which is a "just in case" clause, verify the lack of trust. If someone asks you to sign a prenuptial agreement then they do not trust you. Sometimes it is the words said during a disagreement that indicates that they have a *run back* in place. No matter what it is, these behaviors indicate some trust issues that you have. It also says that you do not trust yourself. If you are in this for the long haul then why are you both discussing your *run backs* before the journey even begins?

Even the most anointed couple whose relationship is designed by God can encounter challenges that may force them backwards. They may speak with the tongues of men and of angels on Sunday and not speak to one another all week. But even if they do not make it to their destination that does not mean that you will not make it to yours. Trust love. If you know that God has given you your spouse and you know that they love you and you love them, at least trust love.

Some of the strongest and longest lasting marriages went through a period of broken trust. They had no recourse, no run back, so they plugged up the hole in their ship, bailed out the water that came in and continued on their course. What are you prepared to do for your relation-ship to arrive at its intended destination?

Trusting love does not mean that there will not be any problems. It does not mean no embarrassing moments. It does not mean a journey void of issues. As a matter of fact there may be more of those when you choose to trust love, but trust anyway.

The both of you need to study love like never before until it is embedded within your core. Study and apply it so that if there is a hole that shows up in your ship, you can look at that person who caused the hole and say, "I forgive you." Obviously, plug up the hole right away. How? Do the due diligence, get the counseling, lean on the Go Team and the Grow Team, pray together, assess and reset, reiterate the course objectives, renew the purpose for the relationship and continuously depend on the Holy Spirit for guidance. Once you clean up the mess, trust and go forward. If you focus on the mess caused by their mistake you may miss out on the masterpiece that the maestro of marriage is molding. Trust love beloved, it will never fail. People will fail you but love will never fail you.

8. *There must be a **desire** to get the **support** that undergirds the vision and mission of the relationship.* The vision is what you see as the destiny for the relationship and the mission is what will be done to get there. Write down your vision and your mission for your marriage. If you are unmarried, write down the vision and mission for your life as you believe at this moment. These can change along the way for any relationship but it is important to know what you see right now.

For example, the vision that I see for my next marriage is a marriage that becomes a Champion-ship Marriage that makes an impact worldwide that will never be erased. The mission is to engage Agaphileros in every possible way to make that impact a reality. To that end, we will utilize all the necessary support we can to undergird the vision and the mission.

But where does the desire for that come from? One area that you will get your desire from is your faith. Faith is a practical expression of your belief in God and His word. Do you believe in marriage God's way? Beloved, belief and desire reside in your heart and the Love Manual says that God will give unto you the desires of your heart when you delight yourself in Him (Psalms 37:4). So the question here is do you delight yourself in love?

You cannot grow a desire for something or someone if you do not spend the necessary time with that thing or that person. You cannot have faith in what you do not know. Grow your faith in love and your desire for the vision and the mission will cause you to garner all the support that you need.

Support for the vision and the mission may look like certain activities. It may include getting involved in a local or international ministry together. It may also be getting involved in something outside of the church as a family unit if you have any children. The children need to know that they are a part of the championship team as well.

Support will also come from your Go Team and your Grow Team. They are going to be invaluable to your own accomplishments. Support will also include setting up protection for the vision and the mission. Take some spiritual armor and get some physical protection against thieves and others who care nothing for your marriage. Support will include getting some preventative processes in place. A ship has life jackets, lights, extra food, navigation systems and so on. Anticipate what might become a challenge and store the necessary things on board your relation-ship.

Above all, learn the language of the Holy Spirit. He is the best support that you can get right now. It is, after all, His dispensation. Praying in tongues will bring all things together nicely and build you up above any challenges that may arise. This is important because just before things happen for you in the natural realm there is usually some type of activity in the spiritual realm.

Beloved, when you are close you must be careful. Some of you are really close to a relationship breakthrough as you read this project. Does it seem like all hell is breaking through against you? Hold your ground because it is only a precursor to the real breakthrough. Do not ignore the promptings of the Holy Spirit. He is your key to the victory.

Finally, let me reassure you that even though marriages are under attack there is no need to be alarmed. Everything that you need to succeed has been provided by God himself. Your job is to come together in agreement for your relationship. Read the Book of Amos 3:3 and do just that. Set the course, pack for the journey and begin to sail.

Take Aways M7

- ✓ When I speak of quality I speak from the standpoint of the most quintessential relationship that can possibly exist or the most perfect embodiment of a Championship Relationship. It is the epitome of excellence.

- ✓ Cheap, where your relationship is concerned, is more about how you view things in the relationship than anything else. A totally cheap person sees themselves as the sum total of the relationship and they are 100% vested in their own way.

- ✓ A cheap relationship has no lasting value. Quality relationships have lasting value. Satisfaction is never compromised by speed. Cheap focuses on as fast as possible but quality focuses on as long as possible. Cheap wants to be there by the next breath but quality wants to be there until the last breath. Cheap will use any old material to build fast but quality will use strong materials to build to last.

- ✓ Cheap today is expensive tomorrow.

- ✓ Cheap people usually break down just after you bring them into your life. They will not work, they will not make the necessary personal sacrifices and they will not initiate the changes necessary for a successful relationship. Why do you think that they are on the side of the road?

- ✓ When you research what is the greatest building tool that a person can use to build a relationship, we have a champion. It is *Love*.

- ✓ Beloved, if you build anything with cheap materials it will eventually collapse. There is only so much duct tape in the world.

- ✓ Broken relationships come about because cheap people use cheap materials to build cheap relationships.

- ✓ Cheap material is easier to handle and easier to manipulate, but it is never satisfied.

- ✓ Quality does not settle for mediocre even if it seems to be the most common choice available.

- ✓ It has been said that opposites attract. That may be true in the laboratory of science but not so much in the laboratory of life.

- ✓ We are all born with the nature of cheap but with the potential of quality, both buried within us.

- ✓ With every thought, every word and every action you must feed the quality seed within you in order to become what you were designed to be; an ambassador of quality.

- ✓ When you name something you give it an identity, a characteristic, a nature as it were.

- ✓ I believe di-vision is really die-vision because a great marriage cannot sustain two opposing visions. When there are two opposing visions, one will eventually die.

- ✓ Serving your spouse is not a chore, it is a privilege.

- ✓ Most likely, the vision for the marriage will already be within the man. The wife will be designed to help articulate and fine tune that which God has birthed in her husband.

- ✓ Do not bring your spouse into your world and expect them to adjust. That is selfishness. That is why it is called marriage and not carriage, marry not carry.

- ✓ Marriage must be transparent before it can eradicate shame. Transparency brings clarity.

- ✓ If you are ashamed of someone's past then do not build a future with them. What you are ashamed of today will come up in a conversation or disagreement tomorrow.

- ✓ Never underestimate the power of the Holy Spirit to keep you away from shame when you give in to His leadership.

- ✓ The Love Manual will be your "keep your behind away from that thing that will bring shame to your relationship" book.

- ✓ Refusing to change or stopping the process of change is akin to giving up.

- ✓ Where you both are will be better off because the both of you are there. There will be enrichment, there will be the feeling of love and there will be an accomplishing of purpose.

- ✓ Nothing that God designs is for selfish gain. Whatever God has joined together let not selfishness pull apart.

- ✓ Trust is hard to build up and easy to break down, yet it is necessary to win the championship.

- ✓ In essence, we build trust by what we say and then by what we do about what we say. If I want you to trust me then I must perform the actions that I have said that I will do in order to be a blessing to you.

- ✓ If you focus on their mistake you may miss out on the masterpiece that the Maestro of marriage is molding.

- ✓ Above all, learn the language of the Holy Spirit.

- ✓ When you are close you must be careful.

- ✓ Even though marriages are under attack there is no need to be alarmed. Everything that you need to succeed has been provided by God himself. Your job is to come together in agreement for your relationship.

MOVEMENT 8

Sex and the Sacrifice

We sacrifice the most for what we value the most. Raise the value of your relationships.

Sexual Sacrifice

In this Movement, we will discover how sex is really supposed to work and how we can get it back on track. God created marriage and one way that we celebrate this union is by engaging in the sexual sacrifice. Sexual sacrifice, you ask? Yes, a sexual sacrifice. When you discover the real purpose for a thing and you line up your behavior to it, you can get the most benefit from it.

In "Agaphileros A", I mentioned how God gave me some revelation and understanding in the area of work, sacrifice and change. Love takes work, requires sacrifice and demands change. In this Movement, God raised my understanding where sacrifice was concerned and He has expanded my perspective of it overall. Now I see even more clearly how vital it is to follow what He is saying about this sacrifice. If you get this, you can be free of all the sexual mess that is in the world today just as others have been made free also. Let us look at God's design for sex.

The first and maybe the most important thing that I want you to see is when God created the woman, He built an altar on the inside of her. Altars are places where sacrifices occur. Her vagina is a place for a sacrifice, a sexual sacrifice. She was designed with the necessary blood for the altar. It is within a membrane called the hymen. When she has sex for the first time, the hymen is broken and her blood is released upon the penis of the man. The penis is the equivalent of an offering placed on, or in this case, in the altar. Many things are represented when they engage in sex, whether for the first time or not.

One thing that we see in the sexual encounter is purification. Hebrews 9:22 says, **"And according to the law almost all things are purified with blood, and without shedding of blood there is no remission."** Blood is a purifier and in this text we understand that blood was to be used as a cleanser for the person who was keeping the Law of Moses. The first sexual encounter that we ought to have should be with our spouse and we both should be virgins. And the virgins said, Amen.

Ok, I know that was a stretch. *I* did not even say Amen on that one. In a perfect world it would be a regular accomplishment. However, we are living in a fallen world that is being made upright by the movements of God. But just because it is hard to be right, does not mean that it is impossible. It is the ideal and we should strive to have the ideal by the grace of God. We already do it in other areas of our lives, why not in this? We strive for the ideal body, the ideal spouse, the ideal kids, the ideal home, etc. Why not strive for the ideal altar or sacrifice?

Soul Ties

There has been some talk about *soul-ties* lately, the premise being that when you have sex with someone you will be sleeping with everyone that they have slept with in the past. You are supposedly making a psychological tie with the person when the sexual sacrifice takes place. Your soul or your psychological being is where your will, emotions, memories, thoughts and dreams reside. This may be a more serious concern to a woman. Why? Maybe it is because women are designed to receive seed, nurture and grow it, then birth it into its destiny.

For them, sex is more than a moment, it is an emotional movement that changes the very fabric of their womanhood. It is a moment of pleasure for her that touches every fiber of her being, head to toe. It tells her that she is the only person he wants to be with forever.

For her, sex should be an event filled with nuances and nuggets, stimulation and satisfaction, and not a brief passing encounter. Spontaneity does not mean a lack of creativity, and neither does brevity mean boring. Granted, sex has been taken out of its true context in the world today and some women are not being led by design anymore, but there are still many women who view sex as something that is very precious. If these women are going to give it up to you then they are bringing the rope to make the tie, the soul tie. Yes, they want a husband, not a gigolo.

Men on the other hand are not quite that emotional or involved. A lot of the times, for **immature** men and boys, its wham, bam, done, and they move on. **Immature** husbands do the same thing. What they do not realize is that even though it looks like it is over, it is really not. Those *little guys* that you released into her are ALIVE! They carry your life at least long enough for an impact to be made. If they get into the walls of her altar they will transfer your life to her. Her body will then begin to adjust *for* you and *to* you. The process of nurturing and growing begins. I am not speaking about her being pregnant with a baby, I am speaking about her being pregnant with you. She now possesses your DNA.

Be careful sir because you are leaving your DNA on

the altar. Your fingerprints may be unique but so are your bodily fluids. Now, when the next guy rolls in to make his sacrifice, whether he is a husband or not, she will be passing over to him your DNA traits, processed and developed, while receiving his; soul ties.

In the Old Testament, even though the altar may have been washed and cleaned after the sacrifice, there would still be traces of the previous sacrifices there somewhere. Every altar bears memories and DNA. Your DNA is embedded, my brother.

Fortunately, God has blessed both the man and the woman with the means to recover from the mistakes made in relation to sexual sacrifices so that we all can now wait for the right altar or sacrifice. Women can purge their psychological being of the men that have visited their altars and men can be made whole again so that they can pass on their life to the right person. Reserve it for who deserves it. Read on for more information on what to do.

Waiting on the Right One

Why should you wait, young lady? You should wait because God has designed your altar for a specific offering. Do not be deceived, your altar is a sanctified place just like all altars are. Today, many altars are being desecrated. Men and boys are raping young girls and desecrating their altars. Girls are sleeping with other girls and desecrating their altars. Some girls are making self-sacrifices with all types of offerings and desecrating their altars as well.

Just because you read a book or see a movie or hear a song does not mean what you see or hear is the right way to experience true love. Think about it, would love really do some of the things that you see and hear? Some people make celibacy and virginity a thing not to be desired as if it is a curse. Preserving yourself for the person that God has prepared you for is the right thing to do. God placed that blood there so that when you experience the love of your husband for the first time you can have that altar purified and sanctified as a holy place.

Sir, God provided the blood for the sealing of the covenant of marriage. The blood on your penis is a sign of the covenant being sealed. It is not meant to be some badge of accomplishment that you wear that says that you have had more sex than the next guy or have "taken" more virginities than your buddy. What do you think happens to those who break covenants of blood? Nothing good and that's for sure.

Your part is to bring the offering to the altar that God has prepared for you. When you place your personal offering in the altar, the blood is released and this marks the offering as accepted and the altar as clean and pure. This is the reason that you should wait. God designed this process to take place when you marry your bride. It should be a beautiful time for the both of you, filled with joy and pleasure like honey; honey-moon.

Brothers, you both are spiritual beings, who possess psychological natures and live in earthly bodies. When you leave your father and mother, and cling to your wife, you both are psychologically and physically joined together. This is the process of you both becoming one flesh, sealed on the wedding day. When you bring your offering and place it in the altar, unity is sealed by the blood and the marriage is sanctified before God, completing the entire spiritual connection. Therefore, what God has joined together, let not any man, woman or devil put asunder.

To the Ladies

Ladies, you must learn how to reject illegal offerings. Be more selective about who you allow into your garden because they just might attempt to make a sacrifice with you. God demonstrated how to reject an offering in the Bible. He rejected the offering that Cain brought to Him in the Book of

Genesis 4. What it really says is that God had no respect for what Cain brought and did not even look on Cain's offer. Cain brought an offering and God refused to look at it because it was not what God wanted, needed or asked for.

Do you want to know how to accept an offer? Know that the man that God sends to you will be a husband and not a baby, a boy, a brat or a beast. He will treat you like a lady and never try to take advantage of you by making an offer before your wedding day. He will have class and be a gentleman.

He will not do the following things: He will not pressure you into anything because one or both of you are going away and wants the both of you to share something together before either of you go. He will not trick you into inviting him over under the guise of some excuse, knowing that you both will be alone in a compromising state. He will not take you to secluded places and force himself on you. He will not threaten to leave you if you do not give him what he wants. He will not try to convince you that he loves you more than you love him because he wants to place his offering where it does not belong. If you have someone in your life that is matching this description or is producing similar scenarios, put this book down and end that relationship right now.

You can be a tween, a teen, a twenty something or something higher, it doesn't matter. You can be a virgin or may have lost your virginity in one of the aforementioned situations. What is done is done, but this moment right now is critical for your future. If you felt a tug in your heart while reading the last few paragraphs, I am talking to you. Stop taking offers and begin to rebuild your altar. God is not mad at you and He will still work things out for your good because He has enough grace in place for your total life prosperity. Believe that.

I feel led of the Holy Spirit to include a prayer of altar rededication right now. I know it is unusual for an author to write like this but I would rather follow the Holy Spirit than follow usual. If you want to rededicate your altar to God with the intent to wait for the right offer then repeat the following prayer:

"Father, I come to you right now in the midst of reading this Movement to let you know that I want to rededicate myself and especially my altar back to you and for your will for me. I want the future you have for me; the husband, the family, the career, the path and the life that was carefully designed for me. I believe in do-overs and right now I need one. Help me to make the right decisions so that my altar will never again be desecrated or violated by illegal offerings. And if I should fall, help me to get back on my feet quickly and move forward. Move the wrong people out of my life and bring only the right people into my life. I give you all of me right now, in Jesus name, Amen." Now take a few moments to worship in His presence.

To the Men

Now I get to speak to the man. The older men should heed this as well. You have read some things and who knows what you are thinking right now. You may have seen yourself in some of the aforementioned situations. Or maybe you are one who has been hurt by a female and have determined that all women are like *that* girl or *that* woman. Did you decide to reserve your offering for that special someone but you are under pressure from others to offer it to someone else? Maybe you have found that special someone but do not think that you can last until that special day. Or maybe some of you have been considering getting a *practice* girl. Girls are not made for practicing on or in like that. Whatever your situation, I have great news for you. God has taken care of the situation and there is grace for you too.

As a younger man, I did not take the time to listen to those few men who were talking to me the way that I am talking to you. The majority of men around me probably did not even know what I am talking to you about today. As a matter of fact, I cannot recall many men in my circle of love telling me anything about how to treat a woman like a wife.

I am sure there were those who knew but I did not connect with them at that level often. I was taught how to take care of my own needs. I was taught selfishness not selflessness. I did not know that I was making illegal offers. However, I am blessed that you have connected with me now and that gives me an opportunity to impart something into you that may possibly help you to have a Championship Relationship. For that I am grateful.

One of the first things that I want you to know is that the woman that God has for you is already being trained to be a wife. Proverbs 18:22 says, **"He who finds a wife finds a good thing, and obtains favor from the Lord."** You are not looking for a woman. Anyone can get a woman, even a woman can get a woman. You are looking for a wife, someone who is designed specifically for you.

Have you ever met someone and you said that she was "wife material"? What makes her "wife material" in your eyes? Was it that she was learning how to take care of a home, or maybe she was really good with children? Maybe it was because she was a career woman and already knew what she wanted to do with her life? Or maybe she just looked like she had child bearing hips (whatever that means). One thing is true for most men, when they are looking to settle down they start looking for someone who is "wife material". Wives qualify for the job before they receive the title.

If you have been making offer after offer and now realize that you should have been holding back your offer until your wedding night, you are not alone. One problem with selfishness is that God has to judge men who desecrate and violate altars if they choose not to accept His forgiveness. Grace and forgiveness is not only available for the fornicator, but for the adulterer and the rapist too. You may still have to face the consequences of your actions but God can and will forgive you for them.

I would be naive to think that every man that read this book was "right" with God (a religious term) and did not have an issue in their relationships. Most of us have a problem *with* God and face challenges in our relationships daily, but can I be honest with you? We as men tend to be responsible for the majority of issues in a relationship that cause failure. Selah (pause and calmly think about that). You have to be honest with yourself before admitting that I am right on this one.

If you feel like you want to be a mature man and do things God's way where your sexual sacrifice is concerned, repeat this prayer with me:

"Father, I come to you in the name of Jesus thanking you for a chance to get my sexual life in order again. I yield my offering to you and ask that you help me to reserve it for the one who deserves it, the one that you have prepared for me. I want to be ready for her arrival and so I give you my body to preserve and keep by faith. If I fail help me to recover quickly and keep moving forward to success. Remove the wrong people out of my life and continue to bring the right people into my life. I am a mature man and I am not ashamed to love the right way. Thank you for my Championship Relationship, Amen." Now worship him for a few minutes.

We know that God is a God of design and purpose. When He brought Eve to Adam, He approved the first union. God also designed both of you with a purpose in mind. Your altar and your offering have owners that God designed specifically for you to connect with. Jessy possessed my altar and I possessed her offering. Unfortunately, most people tend not to see God as a viable option for sexual education today for various reasons.

For some, He is too old fashioned. For others He has just too many rules. Yet others also remark that their body is their own and God should not tell them what to do with it.

Whatever side of the equation you fall on, I do believe that God's way is still the best way. Is it any wonder that adultery and fornication is so rejected by God in the Love Manual?

Understand this before I continue, God does not hate sinners. God loves people and sinners are people. He hates sin because it destroys people. As Dr. Dollar would often say, "Sin will unravel your life." God so loved you that He gave his best to redeem you from sin so that you will never have to be destroyed or have your world unravel.

Celebrate her

One of the meanings of the word "celebrate" means to praise widely. How often do you celebrate the wife that God has blessed you with? When was the last time that you celebrated your girlfriend? I read in a "Maui Jim" sunglass brochure that sunlight travels 93 million miles so that you could *see* every color of nature. As I read that I thought this: the sunlight travels 93 million miles at over 670 million miles an hour just so that you will be able to behold beauty. This is what light does for you; it gives you an opportunity to see the beautiful woman that God has blessed you with.

Tell her she is beautiful every day and mean it. Notice every detail; from the top of her head to the bottom of her feet. Have you ever heard of an eye for detail? Get one, (or two). If you appreciate what you notice you just might get to enjoy the benefits of gratitude. The sun rises every day to reveal color. You should rise every day to celebrate her. She needs that from you. Do not let some other man see what the sunlight lights up in all its glory and pay her a compliment before you do. Be the first to compliment her and she will never crave attention from another.

Some say beauty is only skin deep. That may be true for others but not for you. When God blesses you with a wife He will pack a lifetime of discovery within her just for you. She will be beautiful within and without. Do not just look *on* her;

look *in* her. See beyond the visible to the invisible. The visible over time will diminish but the invisible over time will improve.

Also, celebrate her birthday in creative ways. For example, if she is turning 50, give her 50 days of gifts or 50 gifts at one time or 25 gifts 25 days before and 25 gifts 25 days afterwards. Ask your sisters or cousins or co-workers for suggestions. The bottom line is this, celebrate the woman or wife that God has blessed you with. She may have been through a lot of failed relationships to get to you. She may have survived hell to arrive into your life. She may have survived a deadly encounter or two just to bring life and love to you. She has been designed and prepared to take your DNA, nurture it, grow it, and release it into its destiny. Go ahead and notice her, appreciate her and please, celebrate her. She is a one of a kind and one of a design just for you.

Sexual Healing in the Honeymoon

Let me add this little side note about the honeymoon to those who desire to be married.

Prepare for one. Each of you will have a part to play in it and it could be a very enjoyable and memorable time. Utilize friends and family, online resources, experiences and whatever you can to see what honeymoons are like. Consider also finding out what some people did that were not very wise or profitable for a honeymoon. Start a work-out regimen if you feel like you need it. Get that physical part of you ready for impact. If you are getting a wedding planner, then see if they can assist you with the preparations also. Put some finances aside for the event. Most things cost and some cost more than most. Prepare, prepare, prepare.

Plan one, even if it is to be a quiet time with each other. You do not have to do a whole lot of things if you do not want to, but talk about what you each want to take away from the time together. You cannot have sex for a week straight. (No you cannot). You have to eat, shower and engage your surroundings, etc. In addition, there may be some soreness associated with first time sex, or a menstrual cycle may show up unexpectedly. A lot of other things can happen too. We have human bodies after all. It is better to have more things planned than you can do so that if the mood or ability changes you will still have options. You can still be creative and spontaneous at the same time.

Do not be in bondage to a planned schedule either. Do you know anyone who militarizes a vacation? Are you like that? Wake up to a whistle, have a written or typed schedule, go for a 20 mile run chanting rhyming military words along the way, and all of this before the break of day? Let me give you a million dollar suggestion, lighten up.

Honeymoons should be fun. Honey is thick and slow. The moon is considered to be a cool and relaxing place. The sun is considered to be an extremely hot and deadly place. That is why it is called a honey-moon and not a honey-sun. Be cool, relax and take it nice and slow. The focus should be on the happiness of the wife, and all the ladies said, Amen. Guys, you can have some fun too and you will. Trust me on that one.

Take one, and if you can afford it, take it away from people that you know. The Bible talks about how that a newly married man should not be required to go to war for a year after marriage. This verse is worth quoting. There is a lot of wisdom in it for us today. Deuteronomy 24:5 **"When a man has taken a new wife, he shall not go out to war or be charged with any business; he shall be free at home one year, and bring happiness to his wife whom he has taken."** (NKJV, 1982).

Ladies, I suggest you memorize this passage from the Love Manual. You may want to discuss what your *happiness* should look like over the first twelve months of marriage before he becomes your husband. Let him know that it is a down payment for future constant *happiness* and not a one time or annual event. Now if you can afford a yearlong honeymoon go for it. If you cannot, then do what you can financially without it being a burden.

The whole point of this Movement was to help you realize that men ought to make their offerings at (and in) the altar which belongs to them and not in someone else's altar. Likewise, ladies should preserve their altars for such a time as when the right offering shows up.

Today, promiscuity is considered the "good life" and industries have been formed by it. Yet, promiscuity is a great burden upon our cities, while abstinence is called old-fashioned, louder and louder each day.

One of your enemy's greatest strategies is to deceive you into thinking and doing something that you think is right but is actually wrong. It is the reason for this book and the one prior. Thank God that Jesus brought us truth. Truth dispels deception and brings life. You will not know true living until you are living the life that God has designed for you.

Sex has pleasure but you know that it only lasts for a season. At some point, most people will decide that the life they are living is not worth it and will begin to gravitate towards the life that God has for them. Understanding the **sexual sacrifice** is an important part of that life and I am honored that you read this Movement. Now, put away your offerings and shut down your altars as you receive healing for your past sacrifices.

Take Aways M8

- ✓ When you discover the real purpose for a thing and you line up your behaviour to it, you can get the most benefit from it.

- ✓ When God created the woman He built an altar on the inside of her. Altars are places where sacrifices occur. Her womb is a place for a sacrifice, a sexual sacrifice. She was designed with the necessary blood for the altar; hymen.

- ✓ One thing that we see in the sexual encounter is purification. Blood is a purifier.

- ✓ For women, sex is more than a moment; it is an emotional movement that changes the very fabric of their womanhood.

- ✓ Those *little guys* that you released into her are ALIVE! They carry your life at least long enough for an impact to be made. If they get into the walls of her altar they will transfer your life to her. Her body will then begin to adjust *for* you and *to* you.

- ✓ Every altar bears memories and DNA.

- ✓ Reserve it for who deserves it.

- ✓ Do not be deceived. Your altar is a sanctified place just like all altars are.

- ✓ Some people make celibacy and virginity a thing not to be desired as if it is a curse. Preserving yourself for the person that God has prepared you for is the right thing to do.

- ✓ Sir, God provided the blood for the sealing of the covenant of marriage. The blood on your penis is a sign of the covenant being sealed. It is not meant to be some badge of accomplishment to have more than the next guy.

- ✓ Know that the man that God sends to you will be a husband and not a baby, a boy, a brat or a beast. He will treat you like a lady and never try to take advantage of you by making an offer before your wedding day. He will have class and be a gentleman.

- ✓ One thing is true for most men, when they are looking to settle down they start looking for someone who is "wife material". Wives qualify for the job before they receive the title.

- ✓ Grace and forgiveness is not only available for the fornicator, but for the adulterer and the rapist too.

- ✓ As Dr. Dollar would often say, "Sin will unravel your life." God so loved you that He gave His best to redeem you from sin so that you will never have to be destroyed or have your world unravel.

- ✓ Do not just look *on* her; look *in* her. See beyond the visible to the invisible. The visible over time will diminish but the invisible over time will improve.

- ✓ Go ahead and notice her, appreciate her and please celebrate her. She is a one of a kind and one of a design just for you.

- ✓ Most things cost, and some cost more than most. Prepare, prepare, prepare.

- ✓ Prepare, Plan and Take a honeymoon.

CONCLUSION: Pt 2

The Beginning

Your dream must create a thirst in you that only its fulfillment can quench. Get thirsty my friend.

Creating and Inventing

In the beginning, God, who is love, created the heavens and the earth. Since that beginning, there has been a plethora of things created. Here are some examples. In the late 1800s Thomas Edison created the first commercially practical incandescent light and the world has been a brighter place ever since. In the early 1900s the Wright Brothers created fixed wing aircraft and birthed the modern era of aviation.

In the early 1900s Madame C. J. Walker created a line of African American hair products that enabled her to become the first black female millionaire. In the early 1900s Albert Einstein came up with the Theory of Relativity and $E=mc^2$ and changed physics forever. In the early 1900s Henry Ford created the Model T automobile which revolutionized the auto industry and brought the automobile to the masses. In 1969 NASA created a vehicle that took men to the surface of the moon. The list of those that defied the odds and went against the norm is staggering yet encouraging.

The Love of a Lifetime

We could mention a lot of our modern celebrated achievers in the fields of science, the arts, business, technology, education, service and of course love. Love? Yes, love. I recently came across the story of Floyd and Violet Hartwig on the internet and it brought tears to my eyes (as usual). They were married in 1947 and for 67 years had a special love. He wrote her love letters while he was serving in the US Navy that were deeply touching. They were inseparable. Nothing could separate them, not even wars and sickness. He had dealt with colon cancer and bladder cancer in the 60s while she had dealt with strokes and dementia more recently. However, they stayed together.

When their health declined they were admitted to hospice care. They did not want to be separated so they asked to come home. The family cleared out the living room and placed 2 hospital beds side by side, close enough for them to hold hands one more time. They knew that their lives here on earth were winding up and they wanted to be together to the final breath. He passed away first and then 5 hours later she did as well. He was 90 years old and she was 89. The story is worth your read. Just Google, *"Couple married 67 years die holding hands in their home."*

That was a powerful account of what Agaphileros looks like. But let me share with you another account that was brought to my attention by my little researcher, Avalon (my younger daughter). You can Google this one too. This story was also about a couple that died while holding hands. Gordon Yeager was 94, his wife Nancy was 90 and they were married for 72 years. In October 2011 they were involved in an auto accident. They were both taken to the hospital and were in separate rooms. When it was obvious that their conditions were not improving, they were moved to the same room so that they could hold hands for their final moments. Gordon died first and then exactly one hour later Nancy passed on.

But the amazing part of this story was this. After he died, his heart monitor was picking up her heart beat through her hands. Their son said that his mom's heart was beating through his dad. That is called a poignant moment; it moves you emotionally. Personally, it sounds like her heart was searching for the only other heart it had ever loved and when it could not find the other part of the duet, it too stopped singing. The Love Manual said that the two shall become one. Done.

And if that was not enough, while finishing up this book I came across yet another example of Agaphileros in action. This one you can Google or find on YouTube as well. It is about a couple that was married for 73 years who died just about 5 minutes apart. Their names were William (93) and Lillian (89) Wilson. They both suffered from Alzheimer's disease and both were committed to nursing homes that were 16 miles apart. They last saw each other during the Christmas season on 2014 and died on April 7th. Their son received calls from both nursing homes exactly 5 minutes apart.

Now, you know 5 is the number of grace. The grace of God is sufficient for all that we encounter. His grace is the wind beneath your wings, the difference between your relationship finishing well or falling short. Thank God for stories like these and all the others. These are three of our celebrated achievers in the field of love.

Believe and Begin Again

What do these have to do with the beginning? Well, the end of a thing cannot materialize unless it begins. Do you want to experience the love of a lifetime? Do you want to love someone that much that you both desire to leave earth together after a good long life? Do you believe in Agaphileros with one person for a lifetime? If you answered yes to these questions then I am here to challenge you with these final words; believe and begin again.

The creators (or inventors) I previously mentioned changed the world but they had to deal with people who did not believe in them or in what they were doing. I am sure the Hartwigs, the Yeagers and the Wilsons had their share of naysayers as well. They had to begin in the face of great odds and opposition. Listen beloved, some people will be constant critics and nagging nemeses. They will tell you why you cannot achieve anything including lifetime love. They can usually discourage you with 3 questions: **why, why now,** and **why you.**

Question #1

"**Why?**" They will ask you why you want to do what you plan to do. They are not asking to garner information so that they can help you, they are asking because they want to discourage you from moving forward. *They* want to stop you. They will say things like, "It has never been done before." "No one in your family ever did something like that." "Are you crazy?" "It won't benefit anyone."

Let me give you my answer to that question: **Why Not?** Why not create an automobile that the average man could buy, Mr. Henry Ford? Why not create hair products that can benefit African Americans, Madame C. J. Walker? Why not create a space shuttle to go to the moon and back, N.A.S.A.? Why not love the same person for 67 years Mr. and Mrs. Hartwig, 72 years Mr. and Mrs. Yeager and 73 years Mr. and Mrs. Wilson? Why not?

Question #2

"**Why now?**" When they cannot stop you they will try to delay you. Do not fall into that trap. They like you where you are and when you begin to believe in anything else it threatens their status quo. They like you at that level because *they* are at that level.

My answer to that question is also simple, **"Why Not Now?"** Timing was crucial to all the creators and the things they created. The necessary things were in the earth at the right time for their dreams to come alive. The Hartwigs created true love while he was on shore leave from the Navy and attending a local dance. Timing is crucial to you and God knows that this is your time. You have been brought to the earth for such a time as this. God has big plans for you whether it is in science, love, music, service or something else.

Question #3

"Why you?" It sounds a bit insulting and it truly is. This is the real core of the hater; their jealousy. It is eating at them that you are about to be celebrated and *they* are not. They have every reason in their minds as to why you should be over looked and kept back. They can list your failures and their successes like a grocery list. They are like Job's friends from the Book of Job in the Love Manual. They speak like they will help you to be all that you can be but they won't. Jealousy will always show up somewhere and at some point.

Their questions may breed discouragement and fear into your dreams. My answer to them is firm but full of faith, **"Why not you?"** Are you not one of God's favorite children also? Read to them the following, **"Therefore, humble yourselves [demote, lower yourselves in your own estimation] under the mighty hand of God, that in due time He may exalt you"** 1 Peter 5:6 (Amplified Bible, 1967). Your time to have the best is now, beloved. Take it.

The Promise is Possible

Beloved, you can have what God has promised to you. Ladies, you can be loved like you have never been loved before by a husband that loves you like Christ loved the Church. Gentlemen, you can have a wife that will stick and stay with you no matter what you both face. She will not quit on you. It is not a fantasy, it is our reality.

The Hartwigs, Yeagers, Wilsons, I and many others also lived the dream to the death. Do not let haters, losers, the lust of money, licentious or immoral living, bad habits and wrong relationships ruin a good life, your good life. Turn away from the things that are designed to steal, kill and destroy what is right. Turn to the right way even if it is the long way. Stay on the right track even if you have not received the manifestations of all your dreams and desires at this time. Use Lolo Jones as motivation in this regard.

Celebrated Olympian, bobsled athlete and hurdler Lolo Jones talked about how she trained 6 days a week for 4 years just to run a 12 second 100 meter hurdle race. That equals out to about 1252 days, 30,048 hours, 1,802,880 minutes and 108,177,800 seconds. During the finals, she fell on the last hurdle in the 2008 Olympics. By the way, she was ahead of the pack and had the gold medal all but secured. She ended up finishing out of the medals. Nevertheless, she went back to training and did it all again.

However, in the 2012 Olympics she was not fast enough to medal in the final. She gave up 8 years, 2504 days, 60,096 hours, 3,605,760 minutes, 216,345,600 seconds for 24 seconds of the Olympics and came up empty of medals. As I write this book she has returned to her training regimen again. What an example of dedication and persistence. What a woman. In my opinion, she should get a medal just for effort.

Many of us marvel at the dedication of great people like Lolo, the Hartwigs, the Yeagers and the Wilsons. Isn't it time you added your name to the list? Believe and begin again.

To love like you have never loved before may require you to ask yourself questions that you have never asked yourself before. It may require you to go places you have never gone to before. It may require you to do work, make sacrifices and initiate changes that you never had to before. You can do it; you can begin again, even for the hundredth time. Believe and begin again.

Loving **is** the right thing to do, and if loving (you) is right, then I don't want to be wrong. I believe and therefore I have begun, again.

References

Jakes, T. D. (2014). Instincts. The Power to Unleash Your Inborn Drive. Hachette Book Group, New York. New York.

Rohn, J. (1991). The Five Major Pieces to the Life Puzzle. Dickinson Press. Lake Dallas, TX.

Wilson. R. F. (1985-2015). All rights reserved. Used by permission. Retrieved from

http://www.jesuswalk.com/lessons/5_33-39.htm

THE BONUS

The following are five poems that have been reloaded from "Agaphileros A" just for the agaphilerosos to share with his agaphilerosa, and a vow for both of them to say together. Enjoy.

Kiss

Yes I said kiss, for me it was all bliss, it's what I really miss, as I fall into this abyss,

An abyss of love so true, memories rushing through, a love just for two, falling head over heels for you,

Falling is my new theme, giving up the old schemes, releasing inhibited dreams, flowing in love streams,

Streams of water, that tastes so bitter, without my lover, so please remember,

Remember our first kiss, and the bliss, oh my sweetness, my joy and happiness,

As we begin this trip, fingers in fingertips, hips touching hips, lips pressing lips,

Kissing with passion, the world in oblivion, love in resurrection, eros direction,

Kiss me once more, before you walk out the door, kiss me once more, that's what lips are for.

Winning

It's a constant theme of her life
It's what she speaks every night
And as she wakes in the morning
It's on her lips as she gets going

She is a winner and has no failure
She wins, and that couldn't be clearer
Don't look for her in the gutter
Because she always soars higher

She can give you a paying job
As long as you aren't a slob
Her pockets are full of money
Her words flow like honey

So you'd better come real good
Whether from the penthouse or the hood
This is Ms. Independent for sure
So losers leave, take a detour

You inspire me

I feel inspired. You inspire me so I write.
I feel joy. You inspire me so I sing.
I feel peace. You inspire me so I am rest.
I feel like climbing. You inspire me so I trust.

I feel closer. You inspire me to hold.
I feel growth. You inspire me to reach.
I feel humble. You inspire me to bow.
I feel like staying. You inspire me to wait.

I feel uninhibited. You inspire me to create.
I feel captivated. You inspire me to stay.
I feel enchanted. You inspire me to seek.
I feel like living. You inspire me to live.

I feel strong. You inspire me to work.
I feel my potential. You inspire me to sacrifice.
I feel satisfied. You inspire me to change.
I feel like giving. You inspire me to love.

You had me at hello

I'm not sure if I told you the secret to my heart
But you sealed the deal right from the start
Just your presence is enough for my show
Because baby girl, you had me at hello

I'm not sure if I assured you that all others are gone
Gone like the objects of some sad love song
You're all I ever wanted and I love you so
Because baby girl, you had me at hello

I'm not sure if I said this to you prior
But baby girl you are the only one I desire
You have all of me and I beg, never let me go
Because baby girl, you had me at hello

I'm not sure if love can be any greater than this
'Cause when you're not here, it's you that I miss
So as long as I live I'll never let you go
Because baby girl, you had me at hello

We win!

In spite of the obstacles, the hurt and many spectacles
Don't you know we were created to win?
The long and dark nights, the arguments and the fights
Don't you know we were created to win?

The mistakes, the sorrys, and the forgive me's
Don't you know we were created to win?
Lost friendships, loose lips and the sunken ships
Don't you know we were created to win?

The money that was lost, how we counted up the cost
Don't you know we were created to win?
The prayers and fasting, the seeking and the asking
Don't you know we were created to win?

So forever we will be, together you and me
And for eternity, we win!

A Vow For 2 Please

I _____ vow to love you _____ and I _____ vow to love you _____ also, for the rest of our lives together. I vow to love you without restrictions and limitations of expression and display. I vow to love you until the clock runs out of time, till the end of the line, because forever you'll be mine. I vow to hold you until the winter ceases to come and until the last day of the sun. I vow to make you the only person I will ever long for in this life, the only person that I will ever need to satisfy me, the only one I desire. I vow to be your best friend and I will not put anyone ahead of you. I vow to tell you everything and I will always tell you the truth, even if it makes me look bad. I vow to never hurt you with the things I say, or with the things I do. I vow to speak to you in a caring and thoughtful manner and never put you down. I vow to be appreciative and thankful for all that you do and never take you for granted. I vow to lift you up and promote you into what God has called you to do. I will support your endeavors and be considerate of your efforts. I vow to protect you from people and things that will hurt you and I will always have your back. I vow to protect our home and I will not allow anything to destroy what we have built. I vow to protect our family at all cost and I will utilize all my resources to do so. I vow to cherish you, honor you, bless you, love you and keep you in the one and only spot in my heart. I vow you my love, my heart and my body until my last breath, so help me God to do so.

www.ingramcontent.com/pod-product-compliance
Lightning Source LLC
LaVergne TN
LVHW051117080426
835510LV00018B/2094